THE BEST OF
Birds&Blooms

American goldfinch, page 33

Table of Contents

© 2022 RDA Enthusiast
Brands, LLC.
1610 N. 2nd St., Suite 102,
Milwaukee, WI 53212-3906

**International Standard Book
Number:**
D 978-1-62145-784-8
U 978-1-62145-785-5

Component Number:
D 118500108H
U 118500110H

We are committed to both the
quality of our products and
the service we provide to our
customers. We value your
comments, so please feel free to
contact us at TMBBookTeam@
TrustedMediaBrands.com.

For more *Birds & Blooms* products
and information, visit our website:

www.birdsandblooms.com

Printed in USA
10 9 8 7 6 5 4 3 2 1

*Painted lady
butterfly,
page 194*

*Ruby-throated
hummingbird,
page 153*

Welcome!

There's always excitement in the air when we release *The Best of Birds & Blooms.* This edition is no different. It will have you looking up—often in your own backyard—to watch new friends fly by.

We'll take you in-depth on bird species. You'll learn plenty of fascinating facts along the way. Ever wonder how hummingbirds care for their feathers? Check out p. 61. How about determining woodpecker species simply by the shape of their bills? It's all on p. 15.

We hope we leave you inspired to put your eyes on the sky.

**—THE EDITORS OF
BIRDS & BLOOMS MAGAZINE**

CHAPTER 1

Backyard Bird Field Guide

*Find out which fliers are likely to drop by—
and see how you can lure them closer.*

> "I find mourning doves to be such beautiful, peaceful creatures. This heavenly light accentuated the bird's graceful features."

Patricia Welch
SALEM, CONNECTICUT

GOT MILK?
While raising their young, mourning doves feed them a secretion called pigeon milk from the lining of their crop.

LOVEY-DOVEY
It's fairly common to see two mourning doves cuddling with each other. Mating pairs are monogamous and often stay together for life.

The Most Calming Call

The mourning dove holds a special place in a birder's heart—and ears.

MOURNING DOVES can be found throughout much of North America, but there is nothing common about them. Many backyard birders find their soft, distinctive cooing to be calming and peaceful.

"The birds vocalize a lot and that's where they get their name, because of their mournful call," says John Rowden, senior director of bird-friendly communities at the National Audubon Society.

Muted Markings
Male and female mourning doves are known for their brown and gray coloring, black spots, small heads and slender tails.

"They have an amazing mix of muted tones, with beautiful defined black spots on their wings. You can see an iridescence," John says.

Mourning doves are sometimes confused with Eurasian collared doves or white-winged doves. If a thick black band is present on the collar, it's a collared dove. You can identify white-winged doves by their namesake white wing stripe.

Wide Range
Find mourning doves in southern Canada, the contiguous United States and northern Mexico. You can spot them nearly anywhere—in cities, backyards and even the middle of the Mojave Desert.

They are mainly attracted to open spaces. "Wherever you are, you might have a mourning dove nearby," John says. He adds that very few species are so common both geographically and seasonally. Although they are hunted as a game bird and are easy prey for outdoor cats, it's estimated that there are 194 million mourning doves in the United States alone.

Enthusiastic Foragers
These doves evolved specifically for ground foraging and eat up to 20% of their body weight in seeds daily.

They use their crop, which is an outgrowth of their esophagus, to stash food before heading to a secluded perch for digestion time. Mourning doves also often have a noticeably round breast, since it expands during feeding. Scientists once found a record-holding bird with 17,200 bluegrass seeds stuffed away in its crop.

On the Lookout
To encourage these gorgeous doves to visit your yard, install an open platform feeder or scatter seeds across the ground. Wild grasses, grains and ragweed are a few of their favorite foods, although they will eat larger seeds, including sunflower seeds, and shelled peanuts in a pinch.

Mourning
dove

A male lazuli bunting flaunts brilliant color that stands out amid greenery.

A Gem of a Bunting

Attract these vibrant birds with a combination of scrubby cover and millet.

LAZULI BUNTINGS are named for the lapis lazuli gemstone. With their intense color, it's fitting. Sporting stunning blue plumage, pumpkin-colored chests and white bellies, lazulis decorate backyards in the West. In fact, a group of buntings is called a decoration or mural.

In addition to its blue plumage, telltale signs of a lazuli bunting are the white bars on its upper wing (one thick and one thin), a cone-shaped bill, sloping forehead and notched tail. A female has a gray-brown body with buff-colored wing bars, a hint of blue on its wings and tail, and a tan breast.

"Lazuli buntings are a sister species to indigo buntings, which are blue all over and live in the East," says Emma Greig, the project leader for Project FeederWatch at the Cornell Lab of Ornithology. "Where their ranges overlap on the Great Plains, they are able to breed and hybridize. These two buntings are special because of this hybrid zone, and they are greatly studied."

Lazuli buntings like bushy or brushy areas. "If you want to bring them out of the bushes, put white proso millet in your feeders, though they'll also eat sunflower seeds," Emma says.

In the fall, lazulis migrate to western Mexico. Their migration is unusual because they molt en route, whereas most birds molt where they breed or winter. "They follow the monsoon rains through the desert. It's very moist, and there are lots of insects there," Emma says.

When male lazuli buntings are around 1 year old, they learn to very precisely match the song of older males. "If a bird has an unfamiliar song, the others can get aggressive," Emma says. "Acoustically, humans don't have that fine an ear, but to lazulis, a bird from another territory has a foreign accent."

Males sing not only to define their turf, but also to attract a female. Once paired, the female weaves a cup-shaped nest and lays three to four pale blue eggs. Pairs may succeed in raising one or two broods. They willingly nest in backyards with native shrubs.With the right plants and a bit of luck, they'll flutter to your home.

Female lazuli bunting

"I photographed this gorgeous bunting on a hiking trail in the Santa Monica Mountains. This is one of my favorite spring species in Southern California."

Alexander Viduetsky
VALLEY VILLAGE, CALIFORNIA

BUILDING A HOME
Females weave their nests using common backyard materials and then cement them with spiderwebs and silk from caterpillars. Each nest is less than 4 inches across and takes nearly a week to complete.

APTLY NAMED
Not only does its common moniker have significance, the lazuli bunting's scientific name is also fitting. *Passerina amoena* means "beautiful sparrow."

Mistaken Identities

Some birds are incredibly distinct, with one-of-a-kind features—nothing else looks like them. But for others, a related bird is so similar that it forces you to do a double take. Use these helpful tips to separate commonly confused birds.

Cedar waxwing

Bohemian
waxwings

Cedar and Bohemian Waxwings

These crested birds both have bright yellow
tail tips, wander in flocks and feast on berries.
Bohemians are the more northerly waxwings,
spending summers in Alaska and western
Canada. In winter, though, they move south
and east, overlapping with the more common
and widespread cedar waxwing.

Both birds are named for the red, waxy-looking
tips on their wings, but Bohemians also have bold
yellow and white wing markings. Look for a
reddish tinge on the face of Bohemians, but the
key area to check is under the tail—Bohemian
waxwings have bright reddish brown coloring
there, while on cedar waxwings, those feathers
are plain white.

Ruby-crowned
kinglet

Ruby-Crowned and Golden-Crowned Kinglets

Look closely for these tiny birds that flit their wings nervously as they flutter about in foliage. Both show one obvious white wing bar that is bordered with black. The red plumage of the ruby-crowned kinglet is seen only on the male and is often hidden by other feathers. The golden-crowned shows a patch that is yellow or yellow and orange. For an easier field mark, take a look at their faces. The ruby-crowned has a bold white eye ring, giving it a surprised look. The golden-crowned has a white eyebrow topped by a black stripe running along the side of its crown.

Golden-crowned kinglet

Downy
woodpecker

Hairy
woodpecker

Hairy and Downy Woodpeckers

These two woodpeckers commonly live side by side throughout most of North America, but the downy is a more common backyard visitor. Wearing remarkably similar patterns, hairy and downy woodpecker males both have a red spot on the back of the head, unlike the females shown here. When they're not seen together like this, the size difference between them may not be obvious. A more reliable identifier is the shape of the bill. The hairy woodpecker has a spear almost as long as its head, compared to the downy's short, sharp point. With a close view, the downy woodpecker usually shows black spots on the white outer tail feathers, while the hairy typically doesn't have these spots.

American
tree sparrow

Chipping and American Tree Sparrows

These two sparrow species take turns as popular backyard birds in the northern United States. Chipping sparrows live there in summer, migrating to southern states in fall. American tree sparrows spend summers in the Arctic, appearing south of Canada only from late fall to early spring. The tree sparrow is slightly larger, with more obvious white wing bars. The stripe behind its eye is reddish brown, not black or dark gray as on the chipping sparrow. Pay attention to the different bill colors as well: They are bicolored black and yellow on tree sparrows, while chipping sparrows' bills are black in summer and partly dull pink in winter.

Chipping
sparrow

BIRD ID CHEAT SHEET

Make note of these key clues.

- **SHAPE:** Observe the bird's bill and body shape, as well as the tail and leg length.
- **SIZE:** Compare the bird's size to another known species, if possible.
- **LOCATION:** Range, season and habitat all help narrow down the likely choices.
- **BEHAVIOR:** Be sure to notice whether the bird is hopping on the ground, soaring, climbing trees or doing something else.
- **FIELD MARKS:** Pay close attention to wing bars, eye rings, stripes on the body, and stripes or spots on the head.
- **COLOR:** Any bright or unusual colors might help clinch the ID.

Barn swallow

Cliff and Barn Swallows

Both cliff and barn swallows build mud nests on buildings and bridges. Their tail shape is what separates them in flight—the barn swallow has a long forked tail with white spots, while the cliff swallow's tail is short. When perched, both show reddish brown throats and steel blue backs. The forehead can be white or brown on cliff swallows, but a barn swallow's is always reddish brown. Look for the cliff swallow's pale buff-colored lower back and rump, and pale collar across the back of the neck. The barn swallow's back is solidly dark blue, from head to tail.

Cliff swallow

"Purple finches add a beautiful pop of color when they land in our Blue Atlas cedar trees. They're always a delight to see."

Ashley Maris
GRANTS PASS, OREGON

COZY WINTER FEAST

Attract purple finches by providing sunflower seeds in a cute log cabin-inspired feeder. It holds enough seed to feed a small flock. Available at *duncraft.com*

FILL THE FEEDER

Black oil sunflower seeds seem to be the food of choice for purple finches, but they also eat white millet and thistle seeds.

Winter's Festive Finch

Use sunflower seeds to lure these ruby red birds to your feeders.

PURPLE FINCHES are an absolute backyard treat. Despite their name, they have a hue that's more reddish than purple. Roger Tory Peterson, the ornithologist and editor of the *Peterson Field Guide* series, once described these birds as a "sparrow dipped in raspberry juice."

These forest-dwelling songbirds are found mainly in the Midwest, East and along the Pacific Coast. Look for a bird that is slightly larger than a chickadee or nuthatch, with a short notched tail and a prominent, strong beak, which they mainly use to crack into tough seeds.

Purple finches are often confused with house finches, but purples are heavier with shorter tails and longer wingtips. Male purple finches have an almost completely red face and neck with pinkish red covering most of the body. Purple and house finches don't flock together, but they might show up at your feeder at the same time. In the West, Cassin's finches are also similarly colored. They have a bright red cap, like the purple, but a lighter pink face, neck and upper chest.

A musical bird, the purple finch sometimes copies other birds, such as American goldfinches or eastern towhees, as they sing loudly from the treetops. But when it's time to woo a mate, the male purple finch mellows his tune, hopping in front of the female and puffing his feathers. If she seems interested, the avian Romeo pops a foot in the air, vibrates his wings, and lands to present a twig or piece of grass.

Purples like to nest on the limbs of conifers, though in the southern part of their breeding range they might nest in an oak, maple or cherry tree. The female carefully builds a twig cup, about 7 inches across and 4 inches deep, lining it with grass, moss and animal fur in preparation for the young.

Clutches range from two to seven pale green eggs with brown and black marks, each just under an inch long. It takes less than two weeks for the eggs to hatch. Afterward, both parents feed the naked, helpless chicks. The young grow quickly and fledge in two weeks.

Don't worry if finches visited your backyard last winter but don't show up this year. They migrate erratically. Those that breed in Canada head to the central and southern United States for the winter, while the ones that spend their summer on the Pacific Coast, around the Great Lakes and in the Northeast often don't migrate at all, except to lower elevations.

They'll probably be back again, especially if your feeders are filled with black oil sunflower seeds—a finch favorite.

Purple finch

Male varied
thrush

Voice of the Northwest

A haunting call and fancy feathers make this thrush stand out.

WHEN LOOKING FOR WORDS to best describe the varied thrush, the phrase "dramatically beautiful" certainly comes to mind. Males of this fancy thrush variety sport a bold black band that resembles a necklace on a rich orange breast, a blue-gray back, orange wing bars and a wide black stripe across the eyes. Females are similar but paler. Varied thrushes are about the size and shape of an American robin.

Seeing this species is a treat, since varied thrushes are "not the kind of bird to sit out in the open," says Maeve Sowles, president of the Lane County Audubon Society in Oregon. "You hear them more than you see them."

These particular thrushes live year-round in the wet forests of the mild Pacific Coast—all the way from southeastern Alaska to Northern California. Females lay one to six sky blue eggs, sometimes speckled, in a woven cup often decorated with moss.

Farther inland and north, they are migratory, nesting in forests from Alaska to the mountains of Montana. They retreat southward and to lower elevations in autumn, visiting backyards and parks.

Just like the first robin of spring, "the first report of a varied thrush in fall gets a lot of excitement!" Maeve says. She recommends opening a window on an autumn morning and listening for their haunting and distinct call.

The varied thrush sings a single drawn-out note, then pauses, then another note comes, and so on. "Each note grows out of nothing, swells to a full tone, and then fades away to nothing until one is carried away with the mysterious song," ornithologist and bird artist Louis Agassiz Fuertes wrote more than a century ago in a handbook.

Look for these ground feeders under trees and shrubs, often scratching in leaf litter for beetles, sow bugs, snails, worms and other morsels. "In fall and winter, they eat fruit and berries from trees and bushes, including crabapples, thimbleberries, snowberries, native salals and cascaras, for as long as they last," Maeve says.

To lure varied thrushes, scatter birdseed on the ground and offer suet in a wire cage. "These birds stay all winter," says Maeve, "even in snow and ice storms. We don't have cardinals, but a varied thrush in snow is just as impressive!"

This species is known for being a notorious wanderer outside of breeding season. It's been sighted in every state of the Lower 48, often foraging in the midst of a flock of robins. Look closely and you, too, may spot this beauty.

"I was overly happy when I spotted a varied thrush in my yard, and he waited for me to get my camera. Such beautiful and subtle coloration."

Nevin Hayter
CROFTON, BRITISH COLUMBIA

SPOT THE DIFFERENCE
It may be difficult to tell female or juvenile varied thrushes apart from robins since they share similar coloring and size. You'll know it's a varied thrush if there are stripes on the chest and wings.

FEEDING TIME
Beckon varied thrushes to your yard with an open air ground platform feeder. Available at *duncraft.com*

Carolina chickadee

> "When I moved to North Carolina from New York, I dismissed these common birds. Then it hit me that I was actually seeing Carolina chickadees, not the black-capped ones of the Northeast!"

Christine McCluskey
CHARLOTTE, NORTH CAROLINA

NATURAL DEFENSE
If a predator tries to disturb her nest, a female Carolina chickadee can give off an almost snakelike hiss to scare it off.

HOLD ON TIGHT
Fill this satellite-shaped feeder with black oil sunflower seeds and watch chickadees cling on for a snack. Available at *duncraft.com*

A Sweet Southern Song

Attract friendly Carolina chickadees with suet, peanuts and more.

TINY AND CHIPPER, chickadees are among the first backyard birds that many recognize, thanks to their familiar, distinctive *chick-a-dee-dee* call. But a few things set this flier apart from the others.

Close Cousins

Carolina chickadees are found year-round in the southeastern United States, as far north as Pennsylvania and west to mid-Texas. Their range overlaps a bit with the more northern (and larger) black-capped chickadee in a very narrow zone that stretches from New Jersey to Kansas. Telling the two species apart in those areas can be tricky. Both have black caps and bibs, but Carolina chickadees have duller white coloring on the cheek patch and a bit less white on their tail and wing feathers.

"The easiest way to tell them apart is by sound," says Robyn Bailey, NestWatch Project Leader with the Cornell Lab of Ornithology. "The Carolina chickadee's song is four to six notes, and it has a broader song repertoire than the black-capped's simple *fee-bee* song."

Bug Banquets

Insects and spiders make up about 90% of a Carolina chickadee's diet during the warmer months. The birds also enjoy berries and happily visit feeders for suet, peanut chips and sunflower seeds.

Carolina chickadees' bug-eating tendencies mean that backyard birders should take precautions to help attract and protect them. "This includes not spraying pesticides on our gardens or lawns, and planting native fruit-producing shrubs such as blackberry and Virginia creeper," Robyn says.

Cavity Crowds

Mating pairs may stay together for several years at a time, seeking out cavities in trees. Females build nests of moss, bark and animal fur, then lay about six jelly bean-sized eggs in a single clutch. They also use nest boxes with entrance holes that measure $1\frac{1}{8}$ inches in diameter. Robyn recommends checking out NestWatch's website for birdhouse plans and placement tips.

Though Carolina chickadees are common, recent research indicates their numbers are falling. "It's an important reminder that even common backyard species can decline if we're not careful," Robyn warns. Support them and other birds by regularly cleaning feeders and birdbaths, adding predator guards to nest boxes, and keeping cats indoors. Responsible birders can help keep these fliers happy and healthy long into the future.

LOOK-ALIKES
Male and female Carolina chickadees are very similar in appearance. Aside from behavioral clues and calls, it's nearly impossible to tell them apart.

CHAPTER 2

Attract More Birds

Roll out the welcome mat with alluring snacks and habitats.

Berries Birds Love

These shrubs feed backyard fliers and shine brightest in winter.

1

Blue jay

1. Winterberry

ILEX VERTICILLATA, ZONES 3 TO 9

Few deciduous shrubs produce as much cold-weather interest as winterberry. Unlike most of its holly cousins, it drops its leaves in the autumn, so nothing detracts from the red berries that are favored by game birds, songbirds and waterfowl. For berries, plant both female and male shrubs.

Why we love it: In warmer weather, keep a lookout for Henry's elfin butterflies. Winterberry is a host plant for the larvae of these little fliers.

2. Yaupon

ILEX VOMITORIA, ZONES 7 TO 10

This evergreen shrub forms a dense thicket ideal for a screen, hedge, windbreak and barrier in a yard. It can be espaliered or trained as a small tree or topiary. The red berries brighten the winter landscape and provide food for birds. Female plants need a male pollinator in order to produce fruit.

Why we love it: The shrub's adaptability along with tolerance to drought and disease make it a long-living native alternative to the more commonly seen boxwood.

3. Cotoneaster

COTONEASTER SPP., ZONES 3 TO 8

Whether you opt for a deciduous, evergreen or semi-evergreen type of cotoneaster, it will sport red and orange berries that songbirds will love to munch on throughout the winter. The shrub grows best in full sun or part shade in fertile, well-draining soil. There are a variety of different species, which come in various sizes and growth habits.

Why we love it: It has multiseason appeal. In spring or summer, butterflies may sample nectar from the pink, white or red flowers.

4. Red chokeberry

ARONIA ARBUTIFOLIA, ZONES 4 TO 9

Growing 6 to 12 feet tall, this resilient native shrub does well even in poor soil, tolerating wet and dry conditions. Its color varies with the seasons. Look for small white or reddish blooms in spring, glossy dark green foliage in summer, and red berries in fall and early winter.

Why we love it: This shrub's reddish brown bark and bright red berries boost the color within a cold-weather landscape.

5. American cranberrybush

VIBURNUM TRILOBUM, ZONES 2 TO 7

American cranberrybush viburnum is among the best of the viburnum family, with its handsome rusty red fall color and use in multiples as a deciduous shrub. It grows 8 to 10 feet tall and wide, preferring sun or partial shade and moist, well-draining soil.

Why we love it: White clusters of flowers appear in spring, followed by late-summer berries that feed hungry songbirds throughout winter.

6. Bayberry

MYRICA SPP., ZONES 3 TO 11

Bayberry's small, waxy blue-gray fruits offer winter color that's not red! Plus, the berries feed songbirds throughout the season. Grow bayberry in full or part sun and acidic or sandy soil.

Why we love it: Many parts of bayberry are fragrant, including the foliage and fruit. The scent has historically been used in candle making. Home gardeners can snip stems and use them in indoor holiday arrangements or wreaths.

7. Coralberry

SYMPHORICARPOS ORBICULATUS, ZONES 2 TO 7

In summer, enjoy coralberry's bell-shaped pinkish white blooms, praised for being attractive to bees. Come fall, the flowers fade and clusters of red berries emerge. They'll persist throughout winter until songbirds such as cardinals, chickadees and robins devour them.

Why we love it: It's compact, reaching 3 to 5 feet tall and 3 to 6 feet wide, and a fast grower. Plus, it tolerates shade—a major selling point for home gardeners.

8. Inkberry

ILEX GLABRA, ZONES 4 TO 9

Part of the holly family, inkberry is an evergreen that's ideal for home gardens because it tolerates shade and typically maxes out at 5 to 8 feet tall and wide.

Why we love it: Berrylike black drupes emerge in early fall and last throughout winter until birds gobble them up. The dark green foliage is also attractive throughout the cold months. A female plant needs a male in order to bear fruit.

9. American beautyberry

CALLICARPA AMERICANA, ZONES 5 TO 8

One of the most notable characteristics of a beautyberry shrub is the purple berries growing in clusters very close to the stem. American beautyberries reach only 3 to 5 feet tall, which is perfect for small spaces.

Why we love it: The fruits are attractive to many types of birds: northern bobwhites, mockingbirds, towhees, robins and brown thrashers.

10. Snowberry

SYMPHORICARPOS ALBUS, ZONES 3 TO 7

By winter, snowberry's pale green fruits turn white. Robins, waxwings and thrushes are some of the birds known to eat these berries, but sometimes they fly right by, leaving the white fruits to add interest to your winter landscape.

Why we love it: Snowberry attracts all kinds of creatures—vashti sphinx moths use it as a host plant, and hummingbirds love the pink blooms.

**Baltimore oriole
at orange feeder**

Food, Water & Shelter

Focus on the three key elements of a welcoming wildlife oasis,
and you'll have bird friends flitting right over.

Blue jay

Eastern
bluebird eggs
in nest box

American robin

Summer tanager on beautyberry

IF YOU LOVE TO start your day watching the action at your feeders, you're not alone. In 2021, more than 300,000 people participated in the Great Backyard Bird Count led by the Cornell Lab of Ornithology and National Audubon Society. Any day, you can turn your yard into a destination for birds. Just focus on the big three: food, water and shelter.

Think Beyond Feeders

Common favorites such as chickadees and goldfinches readily visit feeders for snack time, but many others don't. "While feeders do provide a great resource, especially in colder climates where birds may have a hard time accessing food in the winter, they don't feed all birds," says Becca Rodomsky-Bish, a project leader with the Cornell Lab of Ornithology. "More than 90 percent of North American songbirds need insects to raise their young."

A good habitat includes plants to draw insects and provide natural sources of berries, seeds and nectar. Choose native flowers, shrubs and trees for your backyard habitat to maximize the benefits for feathered visitors. Most berries ripen in the fall, just when birds are undertaking arduous migrations that require lots of sugar-fueled energy. Native wildflowers bring in hummingbirds in warmer months, plus insects that provide much-needed protein.

To find the best choices for your yard, shop at native plant nurseries or consult your local county extension office.

Just Add Water

Wonderful habitats supply birds with plenty of water for drinking and bathing. Lakes, ponds and streams are the best natural resources, but birdbaths are a good substitute. Be sure to keep them clean and provide fresh water regularly.

Birds prefer moving water, so think about adding a solar-activated water agitator to your birdbath. In colder climates, experts suggest heated birdbaths that keep the water from freezing, drawing flocks when temperatures drop and open water is hard to find.

Give Them Shelter

If you're wondering why you don't see many birds dining at your feeders, lack of shelter could be the problem. Birds need protected spaces to raise their young, hide from predators and take cover during bad weather. Feeders without nearby shelter can actually put birds at risk, making them vulnerable to hawks and other predators while they eat. To make your feeders more attractive, plant shrubs or trees to give birds a convenient place to hide if danger threatens.

American goldfinch on spiderwort

Carolina chickadee at nest box

PLENTIFUL PLANTS
Birds flock to these fruitful yard options.

BEST BERRIES
Dogwood
(*Cornus* spp.)
Elderberry
(*Sambucus* spp.)
Holly
(*Ilex* spp.)
Juniper
(*Juniperus* spp.)
Viburnum
(*Viburnum* spp.)

TASTY SEED PLANTS
Coneflower
(*Echinacea* spp.)
Goldenrod
(*Solidago* spp.)
Pearl millet
(*Pennisetum glaucum*)
Sunflower
(*Helianthus* spp.)
Tickseed
(*Coreopsis* spp.)

NECTAR-FILLED FLOWERS
Bee balm
(*Monarda* spp.)
Cardinal flower
(*Lobelia cardinalis*)
Columbine
(*Aquilegia* spp.)
Salvia (*Salvia* spp.)
Trumpet vine
(*Campsis radicans*)

Yellow-throated vireo with a caterpillar meal

If you want your yard to be a gathering place for feathered families, then birdhouses and nest boxes are essential additions. Becca emphasizes that it's important to make smart decisions based on the visitors most commonly seen in your area. "Nest boxes help to replace the snags or standing dead trees that are frequently removed from neighborhoods or properties," she says. Different bird species have different requirements, such as hole size, box depth and placement. To find the perfect box for your backyard visitors, she recommends the "Right Bird, Right House" online tool at *nestwatch.org*.

Check Your Yard

Building a backyard habitat can bring great pleasures, and also some responsibilities. "When you invite birds in, make sure you protect them once they arrive," Becca advises. "While we don't want to discourage habitat creation, it is important to ask yourself if you are really helping the birds if, once they show up, there are dangerous obstacles that could threaten them."

Feeders that are low to the ground may accidentally turn visitors into easy prey for ground-based predators, such as outdoor cats. Those feeders can also attract nuisance animals such as raccoons, which may stick around and snack on eggs in nearby nests. Hang feeders high and use baffles to deter predators. Keep your cats indoors—and urge your neighbors to do the same.

Windows are another major issue. As many as 1 billion birds are killed in window collisions each year, the American Bird Conservancy estimates. Add decals, paint, tape or screens to make your windows safer.

Enjoy the Show

As more avian species begin to call your backyard home, take time to learn about each one using field guides and websites. Pick up a pair of binoculars so you can see feeder guests more clearly, or invest in a good camera and take up wildlife photography. Share your observations using online programs like FeederWatch or the Great Backyard Bird Count.

Backyard birding is a worthwhile and relaxing hobby. It only takes a few simple adjustments to turn any space into a must-stop location for curious avian visitors.

Setting the Summer Table

Blue jay

Use these tips to keep the season's best diners coming back for more.

**ADD
WHIMSY**
Find feeders
similar to this
sunflower style
online or at
specialty garden
stores.

Tube feeders
attract a variety
of birds, but
especially
goldfinches.

A red-headed woodpecker feeds one of its young.

Special feeders have spots for oranges and jelly. Orioles such as this male Bullock's will love the options.

AH, SUMMER! Gardens are alive with colorful blooms and buzzing bugs, and your favorite migratory songbirds have returned from their wintering grounds. Natural food for birds is abundant, so many people opt to save a little time and money by taking their feeders down for the season. But definite advantages abound for those who keep birds top of mind and keep their feeders filled this time of year.

Oh, Baby!

Adult birds are busy raising their young during the summer, and feeders provide an easy food source for hardworking parents. After youngsters leave the nest, many adults introduce their offspring to feeders. Woodpeckers show their fledglings how to feed on suet cakes or peanuts. Young orioles develop foraging skills by learning to cling to the side of a feeder. Even if there were no other reasons, it would be worth the effort to feed birds all summer just to watch the young ones. You'll never tire of watching baby birds learn how to navigate their newly discovered world.

Fresh Fruit

Orioles are favorite summer fliers, bringing a blast of color to any garden. The bright orange birds rely on nectar and insects as food sources. The best and safest way to attract them is to offer natural fruit. Slice an orange in half and impale it on a branch. Or offer grapes in bunches to keep birds at your feeder longer—they pick at the fruit and don't carry it off. Fresh fruit also attracts robins, catbirds and mockingbirds.

Jelly's Role

Serve grape jelly in a simple open dish near other feeders. Once birds discover the sweet treat, they're likely to become faithful visitors. But offer just small amounts at a time so that jelly won't become too high a percentage of a bird's daily diet. If you provide just a little bit each day, your feeder visitors will still get most of their nutrition from insects and other natural foods.

Mealworm Feast

Mealworms are a treat for summer birds, but offering live ones can be tricky because they're always trying to escape. A plastic dish with slick, straight sides will slow them down long enough for birds to gobble them up. Bluebirds find live mealworms irresistible and will bring their lovely fledglings to feast on them as well if they nest nearby. It's important to offer live mealworms in moderation. An endless supply might lead bluebirds to skip other foods, and they could wind up with nutritional deficiencies.

An adult eastern bluebird shows a youngster the ropes at a shallow mealworm feeder.

Suet-able Substitutes

Suet has long been a winter standard when it comes to attracting woodpeckers, nuthatches, chickadees and titmice, along with a host of others. In hot weather, however, it melts quickly, becoming sticky and then rancid. Many wild bird feeding stores offer no-melt suet cakes that are formulated with special ingredients to keep them solid at higher temperatures. Even with these cakes of no-melt suet, it's still a good idea to place the feeder where it will be in the shade during the hottest hours of the day.

Quench Their Thirst

A fresh water source is important for all songbirds—and a simple birdbath filled with fresh water does the trick. But the sound of moving water makes it more likely to attract new visitors. Keep the water moving by adding a dripper or a small fountain. Or try a new approach: an item called a Water Wiggler. This solar-powered device keeps the water slightly agitated, sending ripples across the surface.

If birds aren't using your water feature, the basin may be too deep. A simple solution is to add decorative pea gravel or flat rocks to the bottom. Summer heat hastens the growth of algae, so it's important to clean a birdbath regularly. Use a stiff brush to scrub the basin thoroughly, rinse well and refill.

The Sweet Stuff

No summer bird-feeding station would be complete without a hummingbird feeder. We suggest mixing your own sugar water. It's easy: Just use a ratio of 4 parts water to 1 part sugar. While hummingbirds are attracted to the color red, you can skip the red dye; it's unnecessary and may cause harm to the birds. Extra mixture can be stored in the refrigerator for a week or so.

Hummingbirds aren't the only creatures with a hankering for the sweet stuff—ants, bees and wasps are also attracted. To keep ants away, use an ant moat, a shallow dish filled with water that attaches above the feeder. Ants crawling down the wire or other hanger reach the edge of the water and then can't get across. To discourage bees and wasps, use the style of feeder shaped like a saucer with the nectar ports on top. The short tongues of the insects can't reach to the level of the sugar water below.

Seed Snacks

Thistle seed (also called Nyjer seed) is one of the more reliable types of bird food throughout every season. It's particularly popular with finches, and by offering it in summer, you can expect to attract flocks of American goldfinches in their brilliant yellow plumage.

Indigo buntings and lazuli buntings also love thistle seed and will slip in quietly from nearby thickets for a coveted sample of it. In addition to thistle, it's a good idea to offer black oil sunflower seeds all summer long for both cardinals and grosbeaks, and white proso millet for other seed eaters.

Baffling Solutions

Many other creatures wander around in summer, and they won't think twice about grabbing a snack. So it becomes even more important to use baffles to keep these intruders off your feeders. Squirrels are pesky enough, but animals the size of raccoons can wreck a feeder in one night.

A wild bird specialty store can help you figure out what style of baffle to use on the posts that support your feeders. If nocturnal visitors continue to raid your feeders, it might be necessary to take the extra step of bringing the feeders indoors every night.

MORE IS MORE
Use a one-pole feeding station to offer multiple foods. Don't forget the squirrel baffle!

Serve mealworms from a feeder pole mount. You can find them at *duncraft.com*.

> "I keep a small container of them near a robins' nest. I put out a few worms in the morning, and by the time I go inside, one of the parents has swooped them up."

Marilyn Matevia
CLEVELAND, OHIO

WHO'S HUNGRY
Attract these visitors with mealworms: bluebirds, gray catbirds, chickadees, grosbeaks, kinglets, nuthatches, orioles, thrushes, titmice, warblers, woodpeckers and wrens.

Mealworms on the Menu

Add this versatile, protein-packed snack to your backyard offerings.

FOR MOST BACKYARD BIRDERS, there's nothing quite like the rush of spotting a new species or flock at the feeder. To double down on the excitement and potentially attract even more, mealworms are the golden ticket.

"Take a handful of mealworms and toss them out, and soon the birds will be trained," says John Schaust, chief naturalist at Wild Birds Unlimited, a retailer that trains its staff on how to attract local birds. "I've seen photographs, especially with the eastern bluebird, where customers have 25 or so bluebirds on their backyard deck."

Served alive or dried, these protein-rich snacks (which are actually beetle larvae) help birds get the sustenance they need to survive harsh conditions and thrive during the breeding season. Sure, store-bought seeds provide much-needed nutrients, but it's hard to beat the benefits of bugs.

These mouthwatering tidbits attract birds of all sorts: wrens, nuthatches, woodpeckers and more. And seeing as how most birds feed insects to their young, the grubs are a simple way to build up your backyard buffet.

Start by putting out a handful in the morning and evening—about 50 to 100 worms per day—and keep your eyes open for a feeding frenzy. John recommends starting small for a budget-friendly treat, and mixing the mealworms with other food sources. Just as humans need a well-balanced diet, birds do, too.

Live and Ready
You can buy live grubs by the thousand and keep them fresh in the fridge up to six months. Uncle Jim's Worm Farm, a decades-old small business that raises and sells its own worms, recommends that beginners buy the medium-sized larvae, about ½ inch to 1 inch long, to attract the most bird species.

"Put the mealworms in a shallow plastic storage container filled with 2 inches of dry oatmeal, and drill a hole or two in the lid," says Hana Yanello, a farm team member at Uncle Jim's. "Feed them apple and carrot slices and potato wedges. They'll stay nice and happy."

Select a slick, shallow cup, so the mealworms can't climb out. Every worm is a potential meal!

Dried, Tried and True
Dried mealworms are the most cost-friendly and convenient option. However, without the bug's natural movement to attract a bird's eye, it may take some time to train your flying friends to eat this snack. Instead of scattering dried grubs on the ground, try to incorporate the larvae into feeders with seed mixes that are already hanging up.

Eastern bluebirds
snacking on
mealworms

Suet Season

Seeds, fats, fruits, nuts and more can mix beautifully to create a calorie-dense treat for backyard birds. Here's how to serve it up.

Downny
woodpecker

Red-headed woodpecker

Red-breasted nuthatch

FALL OFFERS LOTS of fantastic bird-watching opportunities. Leaves begin to drop, making it easier to see treetop visitors, and it's finally cool enough to set out a favorite treat: suet. A high-fat, protein-packed offering, it attracts both insect-eating species and omnivores while providing the perfect amount of calories to help winged visitors flourish in colder weather.

"At different times of the year, birds may need different nutrients," says Ken Elkins, the community conservation manager for Audubon Connecticut. "Suet can start to be valuable to birds in the fall, not just the winter."

While suet is typically made from rendered animal fat, some bird food suppliers make plant-based options with vegetable shortening or nut butters. The fats are mixed with seeds, oats, fruits, mealworms and more—all ingredients you can try out in your own recipe at home.

When buying suet cakes from the store, shop local or buy from family-based suppliers so you can ask questions regarding the ingredients and their melting temperatures. Cornmeal and peanut butter can go rancid quicker, Ken says. He also warns that nut butters in high heat can be too sticky for birds' beaks. Be sure to check the ingredients for palm oil, as palm oil plantations cause deforestation, affecting wild birds and other wildlife globally.

And while suet is tantalizing for birds, it's great for bird-watchers, too, as it brings new species to your backyard for a closer look. "Suet is one of those feeding experiences that keeps them in view a little longer," Ken says.

When it comes to placement, hang suet in a visible area about 10 to 12 feet from shrubs, trees or another protected perching spot. For feeders with windows nearby, remember to place the suet either within 3 feet of the glass or farther than 30 feet away to keep birds safe from any potential collisions. Also, note that the strong-smelling fat in suet attracts mammals, so keep an eye out for local critters such as deer, squirrels, rabbits or bears, and consider installing a baffle to deter smaller animals.

Ken notes that the suet you serve won't replace a very large part of a bird's diet, since the birds will still poke around and find food throughout their natural habitat. He says, "If you are really trying to attract a diverse group of birds, think about having plants in your backyard to provide birds the foods they need throughout the season and to attract more insects."

STIR IT UP!

Melt 1 cup peanut butter and 1 cup lard over low heat. In a large bowl, mix 2 cups quick oats, 2 cups birdseed mix, 1 cup yellow cornmeal and 1 cup flour. Stir melted ingredients into the dry mixture. Once cool, press into molds and refrigerate.

Brown
creeper

Canada jay

Suet Pecking Order

From big to small, these birds swoon over suet.

RED-HEADED WOODPECKER

Among the brightest suet lovers on the block, these medium-sized woodpeckers flaunt a completely crimson head. They are most likely to visit feeders during winter and are drawn to oak, beech and other trees that produce nuts and seeds.

CANADA JAY

Known as camp robbers because of their habit of nabbing food scraps from campsites, fluffy Canada jays are found in northern forests across the United States and are fearless and inquisitive. These robin-sized birds cache extra food in crevices to help them survive cold climates, and they may even rear their chicks in winter.

NORTHERN CARDINAL

These sizable songbirds have short, thick bills, and both sexes have prominent crests. Bright red males and muted brown females are found in most areas east of the Rocky Mountains and parts of the Southwest. They often look as if they're crouched over when sitting, pointing their tail feathers downward.

Ruby-crowned kinglet

Tufted titmouse

DOWNY WOODPECKER

The smallest woodpeckers in North America, downies can weigh less than an ounce as adults. Found across the country in open woodlands, deciduous woods and even the suburbs, these black-and-white checkered creatures are often members of mixed-species flocks.

TUFTED TITMOUSE

This stout bird features a pointed crest, a rounded bill, large black eyes and a gray body. You can spot tufted titmice in the eastern U.S. near open tree canopies, city parks and backyards—and watch as they whack large seeds on hard surfaces.

BROWN CREEPER

Blending into bark across the U.S., these birds with mottled brown and tan backs keep their white bellies hidden as they spiral upward around tree trunks. Smaller than sparrows, they have a few key characteristics: slim frames, long tails with stiff tips, and slender, curved beaks.

RED-BREASTED NUTHATCH

These compact creatures sport sharp features and short appendages. The plump blue-gray birds may appear to have almost no neck under their black-and-white patterned heads. Find them

FEEDERS WE LOVE

ECOTOUGH UPSIDE DOWN SUET FEEDER

This feeder, made of recycled material, keeps starlings off while giving woodpeckers and other clinging birds access from below. $35 at *wbu.com*

TAIL PROP DOUBLE SUET FEEDER

Designed specifically to give woodpeckers a place to prop their tails, this wooden feeder makes for a stunning viewing station. $40 at *duncraft.com*

FOUR CAKE SUET BUFFET BIRD FEEDER

The shingle-patterned roof keeps up to four suet cakes dry, and the grid design allows clinging birds to easily grab a bite to eat. $22 at *morebirds.com*

throughout the U.S. along tree limbs, creeping in all directions.

RUBY-CROWNED KINGLET

Spot these tiny, energetic birds foraging in a frantic fashion through shrubs and trees across North America. At only 3 or 4 inches long, ruby-crowned kinglets are known for their minuscule green-gray frames, constantly flicking wings, and white eye rings and bars.

CHAPTER 3

Amazing Hummingbirds

*Discover more about these little marvels—
and find out how to get them to flit by.*

Tiny Spaces, Big Rewards

It's true that hummingbirds don't need a lot of real estate to thrive. Here's how to welcome them with even the smallest gardens.

Offer natural food sources for hummingbirds by growing a mix of vines, flowering shrubs and potted plants.

Potted impatiens, surfinia and ivy geraniums are compact ways to attract wildlife.

HUMMINGBIRDS ARE TINY BUT MIGHTY—and the same can be said for some backyards. In fact, small yards can be a gift. Unlike with large spaces, it doesn't take much effort, time or money to transform a bit of yard or patio into a hummingbird-friendly habitat. And an added bonus: You're more likely to have a front seat to the action when the fliers come to visit. Whether you're using containers or growing native plants or both, here's how to welcome hummingbirds to a small area.

Play with Containers

Pots and containers are excellent choices if you have concrete, paved or wooden spaces that you want to jazz up with some greenery. Flower boxes add a charming aspect to balconies, while deck boxes and tiered plant stands liven up decks and patios. Even a side of your house can become a beacon for hummingbirds when made into a "living wall." Consider hanging baskets, too—just opt for large ones, as they accommodate bigger prolific bloomers.

Get to Know Natives

"A container garden is a wonderful way to provide more habitat for hummingbirds, particularly if you use native plants," says John Rowden, senior director for bird-friendly communities at the National Audubon Society.

Petunias, Princess of Wales clematis and Pansy Lavender Flush sweet peas

Penstemon

Consider adding penstemon, for starters. And don't overlook several varieties of native columbine found across the U.S., along with cardinal flower. "The amazing thing about these plants is they've developed tubular blooms over time," says John. "Hummingbirds adapted to sticking their bills into those blooms for nectar, which aids in pollination. It's a mutually beneficial relationship."

John notes that native plants act as fantastic hosts for native insects, too. While hummingbirds are known for their nectar needs, they also eat insects and feed them to their young. "By planting native plants, you are supporting the life cycle of other species," says John. "This helps provide an additional boost of resources for hummingbirds."

Another popular way to attract hummingbirds to a space of any size is with a sugar-water feeder. "Hummingbirds' needs regarding nectar are so

THE FAB 15

Top picks to help you grow a small-space garden guaranteed to attract hummingbirds.

NATIVE PLANTS
Cardinal flower
Columbine
Lupine
Penstemon
Trumpet honeysuckle

VINING PLANTS
Mandevilla
Passionflower
Pinkshell azalea
Scarlet runner bean
Trumpet vine

CONTAINER PLANTS
Calibrachoa
Flowering tobacco
Fuchsia
Lantana
Salvia

Ruby-throated hummingbird at lupine

Hummingbird at gladiolus

specific and quite regular, so they'll always take advantage of those kinds of resources," explains John, who notes that feeders should ideally be used in addition to native plants to help fulfill a hummingbird's nutritional needs.

Change Your Perspective

Look around a tiny yard and you may not see much real estate at first. But the options are nearly unlimited if you just think higher. For example, plant a purple passionflower near a pergola placed over a cafe table. Pull up a chair, and it could prove to be the best seat in the house to view hummingbird activity.

You can also create a privacy wall by securing lattice panels to deck railing. Then coax trumpet honeysuckle, which is another hummingbird favorite, to climb it. A pyramid trellis trained with clematis is sure to bring in birds, too, and has the added benefit of brightening a dull corner of the yard or patio.

John reminds small-space dwellers to strategize the plants they provide to hummers. "Be sure to think about the timing of flowers," he suggests. "Consider when certain plants bloom and space out the cycle so the birds get resources throughout the time period they are there."

Add Water and Shelter

Like most other birds, hummers are skittish. While they don't perch for long, they like places to hide as they zoom back and forth between plants and feeders. So consider a small potted shrub or conifer where they can rest. Many dwarf varieties can be planted in containers.

Hummingbirds also love a water source where they can drop in for a quick drink or cool off in the heat of summer. Consider a mister or water feature with a fine spray (keep it off the ground or near a shrub to provide safety from predators). Your colorful flying friends will love both the sound and movement of the water.

Hummingbird Hot Topics

Watching these little fliers at a sugar-water feeder, it's hard not to wonder how they zip around so quickly or how they keep their feathers so brilliant. Dig into the fascinating facts that answer some popular questions.

What's on the menu?

Nectar is the high-octane nourishment that fuels hummingbirds, but they also need body-building protein. After all, these fliers spend considerable time hunting and eating the small insects, spiders and other arthropods that provide the vital compound. Thanks to hummingbirds' amazing agility and their special physical adaptation that makes their bills essentially spring-loaded sets of chopsticks, they snatch insects out of the air. Hovering, they also glean earthbound prey from spiderwebs, vegetation and other places.

Sweet oozing tree sap has a high sugar content, not unlike nectar, so it's also ideal for hummers—but they can't access it without a little help. Sapsuckers drill holes into trees for their food, creating rows of enticing sap wells. Some hummingbird species then readily feast on the sap from these wells.

Left and right: Ruby-throated hummingbird

Female ruby-throated
at a firebush

How do they sip nectar?

A casual observer might suggest that hummers
use their long, thin, dainty beaks like straws.
They actually lap up nectar with their tongues.
Each bird has a thin tongue that forks at the tip,
springing open to gather fluid; then the tongue
retracts as the bill squeezes shut, compressing
the tongue and allowing the bird to lap up the
nectar. They repeat this high-speed lapping
15 to 20 times per second.

What colors are they?

Hummers vary tremendously in the color and
arrangement of their iridescent parts. Even
among the handful of hummingbird species that
are widespread in the United States, the array of
colors is quite impressive. The male Allen's and
rufous hummers have blazing red-orange throats.
The beautiful male Anna's hummer flaunts an

HOW MANY SPECIES OF HUMMINGBIRDS EXIST?

All the approximately 340 living hummingbird
species are entirely and uniquely North and
South American.
They can live
anywhere from
Alaska to the
southernmost tip
of South America.
They're so varied
that adjectives
from the expanse
of the dictionary
are insufficient
to describe these
bird species.

Costa's

incredible iridescent magenta throat, face and crown. Also remarkable: the closely related Costa's hummingbird, which has neck feathers that taper into long mustache-like points on each side and a head wrapped in royal purple.

Do they bathe?

Hummingbirds meticulously preen their feathers. In that respect, they are like race car drivers who take care to keep all parts of their automobiles in perfect working order. Hummers love to take a shower—or even a bath—to help clean their plumage, and they are attracted to gardens with water features, intentional or not.

One bird-spotter reported observing a female Anna's hummingbird that learned to use the incessantly dripping faucet in the backyard for showers by perching on two turns of the exposed metal hose thread. A few years later, a male rufous hummer started to accompany the homeowners in the garden as they made their watering rounds. The bird would fly in and out of the spray and sometimes perch on the plants being watered to catch the edges of the shower. Of course, hummers visit birdbaths and other standing-water features as well.

Female ruby-throated hummingbird in a fountain

Ruby-throated at a zinnia

Ruby-throated visiting a zinnia

WHAT ARE THE COLORFUL PATCHES ON THEIR NECKS?

With just a turn of the head, a hummingbird explodes in iridescent radiance. Its gorget (the patch of colorful feathers covering its throat) blazes in shades that span the color spectrum, depending on the species. These dazzling colors come from the feather structure rather than pigmentation. Each iridescent feather has tiny spikes that are densely packed with many layers of microscopic structures filled with air bubbles. These structures reflect light, acknowledged Bob Sundstrom, a science adviser for BirdNote, "creating color in the manner of sun glinting off an oily film on water."

Broad-tailed

How do they choose flowers?

Hummingbirds have superb visual acuity. They see color even better than we do, with their vision extending into the ultraviolet spectrum.

Their eyes are adapted to see warm shades better than cooler shades. This ability to easily pick out red, orange and yellow flowers amid a sea of green led to the long-held assumption that they prefer red over other colors. Scientists have since learned that the richness of the nectar matters more than the color of its source. The birds are quick learners; it's nourishment they are after.

What's their flying secret?

No other bird can match the hummingbird for agility on the wing. They're experts at hovering—the strategy most hummingbird species employ for feeding on the nectar of flowers.

Other birds create lift with each downstroke of their wings. In other words, typical bird flight is achieved by flapping the wings up and down. Hummingbirds, however, rotate or twist their upper arm bones to invert their wings and gain lift from the upstroke as well. The result? They are the most agile birds on the planet.

Sugar-Water Feeder 101

Follow these six tips to give hummers the best dining experience possible.

1 FIND THE SHADE
Hang feeders in shadier spots to discourage bees from taking over, as they prefer sunny locations.

2 CHOOSE WISELY
When selecting a feeder, pick one with a wide opening to make cleaning easy. Scrub it once every few days, more often in hot weather.

3 CONSIDER PERCHES
Purchase a feeder with perches to give hummers opportunities for a brief rest, but keep in mind that orioles—also sugar-water lovers—may stop by, too.

4 GO BOLD
Look for red! Hummingbirds are particularly drawn to the color, so choose a feeder with red features to draw extra attention.

5 BLOCK BUGS
Certain insects, like yellow jackets and ants, are drawn to sugar water. To help keep them at bay, install nectar guard tips or ant moats.

6 AVOID THE DYE
Though hummingbirds are attracted to red, skip the red dye—clear sugar water works just fine. The birds will still find your feeders.

In the Shadows

A shady yard can still draw in hummingbirds.

1

PERFECT TIMING

A cardinal flower's peak bloom time is July to September—just when hummers are on the hunt for late-summer nourishment.

1 Cardinal flower

LOBELIA CARDINALIS, ZONES 3 TO 9

The blooms of this North American native have five petals that come together to form a tube. The shape baffles some insects, so the cardinal flower relies on hummingbirds for pollination. Give this attractive plant the consistent moisture it enjoys in its natural habitats, such as swamps, stream banks and other damp, semi-shaded areas.
Why we love it: Blooms in the richest shade of scarlet prove you can have vivid color even in the shadiest corners of a landscape.

2 Bleeding heart

LAMPROCAPNOS SPECTABILIS, ZONES 3 TO 9

Send a special valentine to your hummer friends with these heart-shaped flowers. They are classic companions to ferns and hostas in shade gardens, and thrive in the same cool, moist conditions. Their blooms and leaves fade by summer, so cut bleeding heart plants back to encourage new foliage.
Why we love it: The flowers put on a longer display than most spring bloomers, and the easy-to-grow plants are long-lived, too.

3 Ginger lily

HEDYCHIUM SPP, ZONES 8 TO 11

Ginger lilies offer showy tropical foliage through summer, followed by richly fragrant flowers in late fall. They take to moist, rich soil and are generally hardy only in Zones 8 to 11, but in cold areas they can be overwintered indoors and replanted in spring just like dahlias.
Why we love it: That heavenly fragrance! Growers in the South specialize in various types of ginger lilies, which come in all colors, including white, yellow and salmon.

4 Red buckeye

AESCULUS PAVIA, ZONES 4 TO 8

Spot this shrub in the woods and you'll be delightfully surprised by its large clusters of red blooms. It forms a long taproot to compete for moisture in the understory, so plant it when it is young.
Why we love it: The showy woodland shrub challenges assumptions about what a hummingbird plant can be.

5 Weigela

WEIGELA SPP., ZONES 4 TO 9

Hummingbirds are sure to spot this alluring spring-flowering shrub. Use weigela to fill the transition from taller trees to lower perennials. Extend its interest in the garden with reblooming varieties and those with colorful foliage. Strobe is a variety that offers both.

Why we love it: Early blooms offer a food source to hungry pollinators. Look for new cultivars that may produce blooms through summer.

6 Coral bells

HEUCHERA SPP., ZONES 3 TO 9

Many of the newer coral bells offer fabulous foliage to jazz up a shady site, but don't overlook the draw of the dainty flowers. Plant coral bells where they can enjoy good drainage (including containers and rock gardens). In humid areas, try hybrids with *H. Villosa* parentage.

Why we love it: Each bell-shaped blossom may be small, but in clusters they hold big appeal to hummingbirds.

7 Columbine

AQUILEGIA SPP., ZONES 3 TO 8

Eastern and western native species of columbine, along with many other hybrids, attract hummers to their flowers resembling crowns. The nectar inside each tube-shaped spur rewards fliers for visiting.

Why we love it: Stems up to 2 feet tall hold the flowers high enough to make an impact. Native columbine reseeds itself, creating a colony of flowering plants for you to adore or share with others.

8 Toad lily

TRICYRTIS SPP., ZONES 4 TO 9

Related to lilies but resembling orchids, the shade-loving toad lily is lovelier than its name, with speckled purple flowers on arching stems. Blooms appear in fall, far later in the season than many woodland flowering plants. You may also find this perennial to be deer resistant.

Why we love it: Fantastical flowers invite you to linger in awe.

9 Turtlehead

CHELONE SPP., ZONES 3 TO 9

The funny name is also an apt description of the flowers, which are held on spikes and resemble snapdragons. Available in shades of pink, red and white, be sure to look for Hot Lips, a hot pink bloomer.

Why we love it: It provides color in a tough spot and time: boggy areas in late summer. Plus, it's a pollinator magnet.

10 Columbia lily

LILIUM COLUMBIANUM, ZONES 5 TO 9

Native to western North America, the Columbia lily is named for its bright orange flowers spotted with maroon. The nodding blossoms with their curved petals offer nectar to all sorts of pollinators, including hummingbirds.

Why we love it: With a potential height of 3 to 6 feet, large bright flowers and a bloom period lasting for months, this wildflower is a bona fide showstopper.

Male Allen's
hummingbird

West Coast Coppers

Plant flowers with shorter blossoms and use multiple feeders to attract Allen's hummingbirds.

Female Allen's hummingbird

THE SECOND SMALLEST HUMMINGBIRDS after the Calliopes, Allen's hummingbirds begin their spring migration early. Moving north in Mexico by December, they reach coastal California and southern Oregon around January or February.

"If an Allen's hummingbird really likes your yard, it will come back year after year," says Barbara Monahan, whose property in Santa Cruz, California, was a banding site for 3,000 hummingbirds for the nonprofit Hummingbird Monitoring Network.

Named for Charles Andrew Allen, a California taxidermist, the bird was first classified in 1877. Allen's hummingbirds are about 3 inches long, a bit smaller than the Anna's hummingbirds often found in the same gardens. They're notable for their green backs, abundant copper plumage and shimmering red to gold-orange throats.

To attract these fliers, Barbara includes *Grevillea lanigera*, also called woolly grevillea, among her plants. "Allen's hummingbirds have smaller bills, so the flowers can't be too long. They can't dig into a long trumpet vine," she says.

The usual hummingbird tricks draw Allen's. Set out a sugar-water feeder and a source of running water. Barbara emphasizes having a few feeders in different locations, because the males are extremely territorial. These feisty winged Napoleons will chase away a hawk if it flies close to a favored food source or prospective mate.

To court females, males dive at a high speed while making a buzzing sound with their wings or a shriek with their pointed tail feathers, then fly side to side. Males mate with multiple females. Females build their nests from plant fibers, lichens, moss, spider silk and animal hair. The nest stretches as her one or two chicks hatch and grow. She continues to feed them a week or two after they fledge.

Barbara places feeders in prime locations with sheltered perches nearby so these high-energy fliers can rest after feeding. She also sets out fruit to attract gnats, a dietary staple for hummers. Allen's also pluck bugs and spiders off webs, so "don't be too aggressive cleaning your eaves," Barbara says.

She also recommends a water dish that's about 1 to 2 inches deep and 12 to 20 inches wide, with a constant drip source and a flat rock in it for an easy out.

"Allen's hummingbirds will skitter along the top of the water. Think water-skiing!" says Barbara, who also sets up a mister during the summer. "Other birds like it, too."

SUBTLE DIFFERENCES
Female and immature male Allen's look incredibly similar. Look closely at their throats— a tiny patch of red-orange feathers signifies a female.

TUCKED AWAY
During the breeding season, you're more likely to spot male Allen's near scrubby plants, but females seek out thicker cover once nesting.

SWEET FAVES
Allen's hummingbirds are particularly big fans of these nectar plants: bush monkey flower, Indian paintbrush, twinberry honeysuckle, Western columbine, penstemon.

"I begin each day outside watching hummingbirds. There's nothing like the cool morning air and the sound of whirring wings among the quiet of my rural yard."

Julie Kirk
OBION, TENNESSEE

Eyes Full of Wonder

A recent study reveals all the brilliant colors our hummer friends can see.

Above and right: male Anna's hummingbird

HUMMINGBIRDS ARE TINY MARVELS OF NATURE, catching our eyes every time they flutter by. Chalk it up to the speed at which their long, thin tongues draw nectar from flowers (up to 13 times per second) and to their ability to use their sturdy tail feathers to make hairpin turns.

Still, one of the most interesting aspects of hummingbirds is not apparent to the naked eye. In fact, it was realized only in the last few years. A recent study published by the National Academy of Sciences called "Wild Hummingbirds Discriminate Nonspectral Colors" suggests that hummingbirds see the world in a range of brilliant colors of which humans can only dream.

Science of the Eye

A hummingbird's relatively large eyes are wired to pick up many more hues than human eyes can see. Hummingbird retinas possess four types of cones, while humans have only three that detect blue, green and red tones. The fourth type of cone that hummingbirds have is sensitive to ultraviolet light, which people cannot see. And when the ultraviolet hues blend with ones that humans can perceive, new colors appear.

Of all the colors in the rainbow, hummingbirds love the color red,

An Anna's hummingbird sips nectar at a feeder.

and for a good reason: Their retinas have a more dense concentration of cones, which mutes cooler shades like blue and heightens warmer shades like red and yellow. It's fascinating how a small creature can have such intricate anatomy.

Vision Plan

Having expansive vision helps hummers do a variety of tasks, including finding mates and spotting food sources. And this is especially true when it comes to locating flowers that hold their life-sustaining nectar.

If you're looking to attract more hummingbirds to your yard, plant an array of colorful flowers like phlox, hollyhock, foxglove and lantana. Remember, it's all about the color red, so the more shades of brilliant red you can get blooming, the faster a few new friends may be flying in to say "hello."

The next time you see a jeweled wonder drop by, take a moment not only to welcome the visitor with a variety of appealing nectar sources but also to appreciate and imagine the spectacular colors that it recognizes out in nature.

FIELD TEST
How researchers proved an ultraviolet theory.

A team of scientists performed outdoor experiments with wild hummingbirds to test how well they see different ultraviolet colors. They engineered special LED tubes that emitted several colors, both on the visible and ultraviolet (UV) spectrum. Then they placed the LED tubes next to two feeders. The feeder with plain water gave off visible light, and the one with sugar water gave off UV light.

The scientists were able to train hummingbirds to associate the UV light with the reward of sugar water, and the regular light with the plain water. When they rearranged the placement of the feeders, similar to the Pavlovian dog experiment, the birds were still more quickly drawn to the feeder giving off ultraviolet light—which proved that they could ultimately tell the difference between the one emitting the special rays and the normal feeder.

DO YOUR OWN EXPERIMENT
Citizen science projects such as eBird, Backyard Bird Count and NestWatch are looking for birders and gardeners to provide valuable data for researchers. Visit their websites to look up opportunities and see how you can lend a scientific helping hand.

SUGAR-WATER RECIPE

Fill feeders with this easy, expert-approved formula.

1. Combine 4 parts hot water to 1 part refined white sugar. Consider using boiling water if you have poor water quality or are storing it for later.
2. Mix until the sugar is completely dissolved.
3. Set aside to cool. Once it's room temperature, pour it into a feeder or store in the fridge for up to 2 weeks.

WHAT TO SKIP

Leave these ingredients out of homemade sugar-water:

Brown sugar

Honey

Powdered sugar

Artificial sweeteners

Red dye

Backyard Sweet Shop

With these feeder tips and tricks, plus native plants, you'll draw hummer friends for dinner.

HUMMINGBIRDS ARE TRULY BRILLIANT GUESTS. Make sure you're sending them a vibrant invitation. Fortunately, it's easy to draw these flying gems to your garden with fuel-providing feeders and native plants.

Anusha Shankar, a postdoctoral fellow conducting research at the Cornell Lab of Ornithology, explains why these magnificent birds are always on the hunt. She says, "Hummingbirds need to eat constantly because they use up energy very quickly. If we had their metabolic rate, we'd need to eat 300 hamburgers a day to survive!"

Nectar feeders are a popular choice. Put them out a few weeks before hummingbirds are expected in the spring, and leave them up until the birds head south again in the fall. In areas where hummers are year-round residents, you can feed them throughout the seasons. To draw more visitors, try setting up extra feeders. The males are extremely territorial, so space the feeders at least 15 feet apart and out of sight of each other, if possible.

Saucer-shaped feeders with multiple ports are easy to clean, making them a favorite style. Most feature a splash of red, since that's a hummer's favorite color. Just don't be tempted to add red coloring to your nectar. Anusha notes that it's potentially toxic to hummingbirds and unnecessary.

It's vital to clean your feeders and replace any remaining sugar water every few days, and more often in hot climates. "Hummingbirds can get sick at dirty feeders," Anusha says. "If you see black gunk growing in your feeders and you can't keep them clean, it's better to take them down." Sanitize them with hot water and a weak vinegar or bleach solution, rinsing well. Skip the dish soap, as it can leave a residue.

Also, to see more of these fliers, provide plenty of native nectar plants that will supply shelter and help attract the small insects hummingbirds rely on for protein. Tube-shaped red and orange flowers, like honeysuckle or trumpet creeper, are common hummer favorites. Visit your local native plant nursery and ask for suggestions for your area.

Like all animals, hummers need fresh water for drinking and bathing. They especially love to play in water mists and sprays, so add a small solar-powered fountain to your birdbath to see them in action.

Hummingbirds bring their own special magic wherever they go. Once you start feeding these brilliant little birds, you'll find your garden filled with a sparkling dose of color and life.

Female ruby-throated
hummingbird

CHAPTER 4

Birds in Depth

Grow your know-how about top species and their habits.

Pairing Up

Learn eight surprising facts about birds' quirky and sweet courtship displays.

Sandhill cranes in the midst of their famous mating dance.

SHOWING LOVE WITH FOOD

A cedar waxwing pair cozies up on a branch, passing a berry back and forth until one of them swallows it.

A male northern cardinal feeds a female, proving that he's able to care for a family.

WHEN BIRDS COUPLE UP, it's not by chance. Instead, some species pull out all the stops to impress a potential mate—from feeding and preening to elaborate dances and feather displays. It's truly a dating game like no other. See for yourself: These adorable photos and impressive truths reveal what bird courtship is really like.

1. There's no guarantee.

Not all birds breed every season. Competition for food, territory and nesting sites is fierce, so when individuals are unable to secure the necessities, they end up missing the opportunity to find a mate and raise a family.

2. Feeding is a love language.

Courtship feeding behaviors are more than kind gestures. Males go out of their way to feed females, and it's typically to prove that they are capable of providing for her and their future

young. Look for this common ritual in your yard among northern cardinals, cedar waxwings and tufted titmice.

3. It starts with a song.

When you hear a bird singing in spring, it's likely a male trying to grab the attention of a female. When a female's interest is piqued by the tune, she checks out the male's plumage to determine whether he has desirable genes, and then explores his territory. If she likes what she sees, she'll choose that male as her mate.

4. Group settings are successful.

Some birds form pairs in a lek, an area where males of a certain species gather to flaunt and perform for females. For example, sharp-tailed grouse stick their pointed tails up, aim their wings down and inflate the purple air sacs along their necks. Sage grouse inflate the air sacs on their chests. The gals wander through the lek, watch the displays and select a mate.

5. Monogamy isn't a given.

About 90% of birds are monogamous—socially, that is! Until DNA fingerprinting techniques were developed in the 1980s, scientists presumed that birds were faithful at least for a season. But new DNA data shows that some of your favorite songbirds stray while still remaining dutiful and doting parents.

FALLING HEAD OVER TALONS

In an interesting ritual called cartwheeling, mated bald eagles lock their talons in flight and then free-fall through the air together.

MATES FOR LIFE

These birds are in it for the long haul.

Laysan albatross

California condor

Whooping crane

Bald eagle

Black vulture

Atlantic puffin

Mute swan

Osprey

FINDING EACH OTHER AGAIN
A dunlin pair may reconnect at their breeding grounds after separating for the migration season.

6. Vibrant color matters.

Plumage color and brightness may be related to mate selection. It's no coincidence that males of many species are at their most vibrant during courtship season. Think indigo buntings, scarlet tanagers and American goldfinches. The color and intensity of a male's breeding plumage may influence a female's choice.

7. There's back and forth.

Come migration season, some pairs go their separate ways. But when it's time to breed, they reunite. Studies prove that individual birds recognize each other when they return to the breeding grounds. This is true for migratory birds like dunlin and osprey and for various species of gulls, terns and seabirds.

8. Courtships are wow-worthy.

Both male and female western grebes participate in courtship rituals. The pairs—or possibly two males trying to wow females—participate in an extremely elaborate walk-on-water display called rushing. Perfectly in sync, the grebes run as far as 66 feet across the water with their necks curved and their wings up and back.

STAYING IN SYNC
Courting American avocets (left) execute a graceful ritual of bowing, posturing and preening. A pair of western grebes (shown here) perform a courtship dance called rushing.

Wonderful World of Warblers

Warblers are perhaps the most colorful and awe-inspiring birds around, even if they can be tricky to track down. Of the more than 50 species in North America, these 10 deserve special accolades—and your undivided attention.

American redstart

A male yellow warbler on a winter king hawthorn belts a familiar melody.

◀ FLASHIEST FEATHERS

American redstarts stand out, not just for their brilliantly bright feathers but also for the way they put those feathers to use. Redstarts fan out their tails in a display thought to startle insect prey into the open. These birds can show up nearly anywhere during their migration, with the exception of the far West, and they nest in parks and woodlots throughout most of North America. Their bold patterns and behaviors are nearly impossible to miss.

▲ MOST FAMILIAR SONG

Step outside in summer and you might hear this whistled tune: *Sweet, sweet, sweet, I'm so sweet.* Yellows, our most widespread warbler, sing while nesting across much of the United States and Canada, especially in shrubland and woodland thickets. Females are pale lemon in color, while males sport bold orange streaks along their chests. Another familiar tune comes from the common yellowthroat warbler as it calls *wichity, wichity, wichity* from the marshes.

Yellow-rumped warbler on a suet feeder

▲ BIGGEST FEEDER FAN

Warblers rely heavily on bugs, but you can sometimes entice yellow-rumped warblers with suet feeders. Some of the last to head south in fall, these warblers shift to eating berries in the southern states. They return north very early in spring. Try adding water features to the landscape to help lure these birds to your yard. You may also attract orange-crowned or pine warblers.

▶ CLASSIEST

The color contrast of black-and-white warblers gives them a look of sophistication. Their methodical feeding style adds yet another touch of class. Black-and-white warblers mimic nuthatches by creeping along tree trunks and branches in search of invertebrate snacks. They're widespread east of the Rockies, and a few show up in the West each year.

Black-and-white warbler

You can find black-throated blue warblers in scrubby areas throughout the East during their migration.

▲ BEST DRESSED

Warblers often sport yellow feathers, but the plumage of black-throated blue warblers would make a stunning prom ensemble. The formal black-and-white "tuxedo" is accented with rich blues in males, while females show a blush of faint indigo. White patches in the wings remind many birders of pocket squares. Black-throated blue warblers thrive in the dense forest understory from the southern Appalachians to the Canadian Maritime Provinces and Quebec.

Kirtland's warbler

RAREST

Only a few thousand Kirtland's warblers are found in the world. The majority nests in central Michigan's jack pine forests, with populations expanding into Wisconsin and Ontario. Each year during migration, a few are spotted between their breeding ranges and their wintering habitats in the Bahamas. Even more localized in the United States, the Colima warbler has a very limited range in West Texas but is more widespread in Mexico.

Colima warbler

Ovenbird with its young

▲ LEAST TYPICAL

Admittedly, ovenbirds don't quite look the part of a warbler. Their olive-brown backs are offset by streaks on their bellies. A splash of deep orange running along the tops of their heads gives each a racing stripe of color. Behaviorally, ovenbirds aren't your everyday warbler, either. They spend their time foraging along the forest floor. They even build dome-shaped nests, for which they are named, directly on the ground.

▶ FARTHEST FLIER

Most warblers are long-distance migrants, but blackpolls take it to the extreme. Some of these songbirds summer in Alaska and winter as far south as Brazil. Each weighs about as much as a ballpoint pen, yet in fall they complete their epic journeys, flying nonstop from the eastern seaboard to northern South America. Blackpolls gorge on insects to build up fat reserves to fuel their three-day trip.

Blackpoll warbler

Lucy's warbler

TOP NEST SCOUT

Lucy's warblers live in the very driest climates. Found in the Desert Southwest, they happen to be one of the only warblers to nest in tree cavities. (Prothonotary warblers, also cavity nesters, live in an opposite habitat: swamps and wet forests in the East.) Lucy's seek abandoned woodpecker holes, natural tree cavities or specially designed triangle-style nest boxes.

WEEK OF WONDER

Held in the "warbler capital of the world," northwestern Ohio, the Biggest Week in American Birding is an annual celebration that gets eyes to the sky. It happens in mid-May during spring migration, when over 35 warbler species are regularly found in the region. Loved by longtime birders, it's also a great introduction to the world of warblers. Learn more at *biggestweekinamericanbirding.com*.

Prothonotary warbler near a tree cavity

Townsend's warblers can be spotted west of the Rocky Mountains.

▲ BEST IN THE WEST

The West has less warbler diversity, but a number of species do appear in the region. West of the Rocky Mountains, the stunning Townsend's warbler is fairly common during migration. It breeds in wet evergreen forests from Idaho to Alaska and winters along the West Coast, inland in Arizona and Texas, and south into Mexico and Central America. Similar in appearance and closely related, hermit warblers mate and hybridize with Townsend's where their ranges overlap.

Blue-
headed
vireo

Summer-Long Singers

Yellow-throated vireo

Vireos may be inconspicuous, but they're everywhere during the warmer months. All you have to do: Look up and listen.

Red-eyed vireo

Hutton's vireo

Cassin's vireo

Plumbeous vireo

OFTEN HEARD BUT seldom seen. That's a perfect description of vireos. This family's members are found all over North America in the warmer months, and about a dozen vireo species are widespread north of the Mexican border. Their sweet songs are among the most familiar sounds of late spring and summer, but the birds are actually very good at staying out of sight among the foliage. It's worth the effort to get to know this melodic family.

Persistent Treetop Singers

The red-eyed vireo is a noteworthy summer bird found across the eastern United States and most of southern Canada. Although it is widespread, it hides high in trees, moving slowly among the leaves. Plain colors—olive above, white below, with just a couple of black stripes on the face— make it even harder to spot. But a red-eyed vireo is easy to hear, because the males sing almost incessantly in late spring and summer, even on hot afternoons.

A red-eyed vireo's song is a series of short, whistled notes separated by pauses. The *swee?... sooyup... sissewit... swiswi* sounds like a choppy version of a robin's voice and goes on and on. An old nickname for this species was "preacher bird,"

perhaps applied by someone who thought the Sunday service dragged on too long. Red-eyed vireos live mainly in deciduous forests, but they are heard in towns and suburbs with enough mature trees.

The warbling vireo, all grayish and white with a pale eyebrow, is plainer in appearance than the red-eyed. In summer it's found in woodlands from coast to coast, but like the red-eyed it spends the winter deep in the tropics. Its song is very different. As the name suggests, the male makes a short, musical warbling, not a series of separate notes. He sings all day, even when he's sitting on the nest incubating eggs. The nest, as with most vireos', is a shallow cup, often suspended in a twig's fork.

Bell's vireo

Warbling vireo

White-eyed vireo

Species with Spectacles

Some vireos are boldly marked, with contrasting wing bars and vibrant eye-rings that resemble a pair of glasses. One example, the blue-headed vireo, spends the summer in the mixed forests of eastern Canada, the northeastern states and the Appalachians. It wears a colorful pattern with its blue-gray head, green back, yellow sides, and white throat and chest.

The Cassin's vireo of the Pacific Northwest looks like a duller version of the blue-headed, while the plumbeous vireo of the Rockies has a similar pattern but entirely in lead-gray and white. At one time, all three vireos were classified as the same species, called the solitary vireo. All three sing short, whistled phrases like the red-eyed, although the western ones have a rough, husky undertone.

The yellow-throated vireo is even more colorful. Its vibrant, bright yellow throat and yellow eyeglass-like markings are quite distinctive. It is found during the summer in eastern oak forests, especially in the southeastern states. The short phrases of its song have a hoarse, buzzy quality, and its slow, lazy cadence is a perfect soundtrack for hot summer afternoons.

The smallest of the spectacled type is Hutton's vireo, a year-round resident of oaks along the Pacific coast and in the Southwest. Tiny and active, it's sometimes confused with the ruby-crowned kinglet, a completely unrelated bird. Hutton's is drab gray, and it may have the most monotonous song of any vireo, just a single slurred note repeated over and over.

Lurkers in the Thickets

Not all vireos dwell high in the trees. Some prefer dense, low cover close to the ground. Thickets in the southeastern states ring with the quick, snappy songs of white-eyed vireos, sometimes written out as *chip-o-de-white-oak!* or *pick-up-a-real-chick!* Eventually this vireo may come out to the edge of the shrubbery to look around, its staring white eyes giving it a surprised expression.

Black-capped
vireo

Another thicket dweller, found mostly in the Southwest and Great Plains, is the drab but active Bell's vireo. Its song is a clinking *cheedle-cheedle-chee? cheedle-cheedle-chew!* as if the Bell's is asking and then answering the same question over and over.

Attracting Vireos

Unfortunately, vireos almost never visit any bird feeders. In spring and summer their diet is almost exclusively insects, especially caterpillars, so the best way to attract them is to have plenty of native plants in your yard and to avoid using pesticides that would kill off the insects the birds need to survive. If you have room to plant trees, oaks native to your area are a good bet for supporting the vireo family.

Before they migrate south in late summer and early fall, vireos consume many berries. Native dogwoods, elderberries and Virginia creeper are among their favorites, and even the treetop dwellers come down to eye level to feast on these fruits. Another way to lure migrating vireos is to provide water. A shallow bath with a source of movement, such as a dripper or small fountain, may be just the thing to catch their attention. However you attract vireos, it's worth the effort to make the acquaintance of these secretive but reliable songsters.

A RARE VIREO

One of the most beautiful vireos is also the rarest of the group: the black-capped vireo, with its black hood, white spectacles and red eyes. A scarce summer resident of scrub oak thickets in Texas and southern Oklahoma, its numbers have declined due to loss of habitat and the impact of cowbirds laying their eggs in vireos' nests. Conservation work by the U.S. Army at Fort Hood, Texas, has helped to sustain good habitat for this vireo.

Because snowy owls hunt on the ground, they prefer open, treeless spaces.

Seek Out Snowies

Learn how modern technology has recently provided answers about this elusive owl species.

ADVENTUROUS BIRDERS LOVE the thrill of discovering a snowy—and it takes only one glance to understand why this owl species is so special. Thanks to research being done by Project SNOWstorm and others, we now know more about snowy owls and their habits than ever before.

"Why study them? I mean, just look at them!" says Scott Weidensaul, one of the founders and researchers at Project SNOWstorm. "They're big and beautiful and charismatic. They are one of the most entrancing and intriguing owls in the world."

Featuring unique markings, which vary widely in color from brown to black and in shape from bars to spots, snowy owls are best known for their white plumage and feline-looking yellow eyes. Scott says, "A friend of mine likes to say, 'Regardless of what part of the snowy owl's life history you're talking about, it didn't read the rule book.'"

In celebration of this beautiful bird, here are answers to some of your biggest questions about snowy owls.

A prominent snowy owl feature is large yellow catlike eyes, as seen in the juvenile (left) and adult (right).

A male snowy owl delivers a lemming to a female in her nest.

Where Are Snowies Found?

In the lower 48 states, the best time to see a snowy owl is during an irruption. This can happen in winter when the owls unexpectedly travel farther south than normal, usually into the northern U.S. But they've been spotted as far south as Florida a few times during rare mega-irruptions.

Surprisingly, these movements are actually not connected to a lack of food. Scientists have observed that irruptions occur in winters after lemmings and voles were plentiful in the snowy

owls' tundra breeding grounds, leading to a boom in the snowy owl population.

A single owl hunts all day in the Arctic daylight and often consumes more than 1,500 lemmings per year. The owls also eat grebes, songbirds, loons, snow geese and great blue herons.

In summer, when populations of lemmings and voles surge in the north, female snowies can lay as many as 11 eggs in a season. Scott once saw five snowy owl eggs in the middle of a nest, surrounded by 78 dead lemmings and voles.

A snowy owl pair surveys together.

Female snowy owls are typically slightly larger than their male counterparts.

What's Too Close?

If you've had the good fortune to see a snowy owl in the wild, you may have noticed that it seemed calm. Some even say you can get within arm's reach of a juvenile. Snowies live in open areas such as farms, grasslands and seashores, often in close proximity to people. While these birds are generally relaxed around humans, they're known to be extremely territorial with other species. If you see a snowy owl in person, remember: If the owl is looking directly at you, you're too close.

Why Airports?

Some snowy owls tend to hang out near and around airports, drawn to the open areas. This dangerous behavior makes it easy for owls to get hit or killed by backwash from an airplane engine. Members of Project SNOWstorm often trap and remove snowies from airports across the country.

How Many Snowies Exist?

Far fewer snowy owls exist than was previously thought. The total snowy owl population was once estimated to be about 300,000 worldwide, but in reality it is actually closer to 30,000. (For comparison, the global population of black-capped chickadees is an estimated 41 million, according to Partners in Flight, a network of organizations dedicated to bird conservation.) The reason for the change in estimate? Because snowy owls travel thousands of miles between breeding seasons, individual birds were often counted more than once prior to the use of modern tracking technology.

How Big Are They?

These birds are quite large and can be spotted from very far away. While snowies are often surprisingly light in weight, they are actually the heaviest owls in North America. With a height of 2½ feet, a wingspan of 5 feet and an average weight of 4 to 5 pounds, they are also one of the most powerful owls in the United States. Their extra body mass makes them a pound heavier than the great horned owl and twice the weight of a great gray owl.

SCIENCE AND SNOWY OWLS

A look into a fascinating research effort.

PROJECT SNOWSTORM helps track the movements of snowy owls using cutting-edge technologies to log the precise latitude, longitude and altitude of tagged birds as frequently as every six seconds. Since 2013, Project SNOWstorm has become one of the world's largest collaborative research projects.

This project is funded entirely by the public and has tracked more than 90 snowy owls across the Dakotas, the Great Lakes, New England, the mid-Atlantic states and southern Canada. Its largely volunteer team consists of scientists, bird banders and wildlife veterinarians from across the country.

Its latest efforts include tagging and tracking owls on the Great Plains and studying how the construction of wind turbines affects these birds. In addition, the group is researching the mortality and movements of juveniles, while also working with airport authorities to relocate owls that end up in harm's way.

Project SNOWstorm assisted Ohio's Black Swamp Bird Observatory with tagging Wolverine, a snowy owl rescued from a Michigan airport.

Junco
Family Tree

Meet the many variations of this beloved
snowbird and popular wintertime visitor.

Female Oregon junco

Slate-colored
junco

Slate-colored junco

WEARING SUBTLE HUES of gray, brown and white, with round little bodies and sweet expressions, dark-eyed juncos are among our most-beloved birds. Since they appear to carry gray storm clouds on their backs and white snow on their bellies, they are often referred to as snowbirds. But they also earn this nickname because of the rhythm of their southerly migration. They fly into many areas just in time to usher in winter snows. The arrival of little flocks of juncos is something to look forward to, even if winter follows closely behind.

The Most Widespread Junco

Of all the dark-eyed juncos, the subspecies with the widest range is the slate-colored junco. These birds are found in summer across the majority of Alaska and Canada, south into the northeastern states and the Appalachians, and even as far south as Georgia. In the winter months they are common from southern Canada to the Gulf states, mostly east of the Rockies but with a few scattered throughout the West.

With their basic shades of gray and white, they are the least colorful of the juncos, but they are still beautiful in their simplicity. They share some similarities with other juncos, such as the white outer tail feathers that are obvious when they fly. In addition, they almost always build their nests on the ground, usually in a spot well hidden under shrubs or overhanging branches. And, like other juncos, they form small flocks in winter, often joining with other birds, such as white-throated sparrows or American tree sparrows. They fit in well with these birds because juncos are actually members of the sparrow family, despite their different color pattern.

For their winter habitat, juncos favor partially open areas, including the edges of woods and suburban backyards. They are readily attracted to feeders with white proso millet, sunflower chips and other types of high-quality seeds. They are most likely to use open-tray feeders close to the ground and often just forage on the ground underneath the feeders.

Along the Oregon Trail

While the slate-colored type is the standard junco throughout the East and the far North, the most widespread form in the West is the Oregon junco. Birds in this category have a nesting range that stretches from southeastern Alaska through western Canada, to Idaho and Wyoming, and south throughout the West Coast states. In Washington, Oregon and California, Oregon juncos can be found in summer both in the high mountains and along the coast. They readily adapt to nesting in parks and gardens, so they're year-round backyard birds in many places where the "snowbird" nickname really doesn't apply.

Oregon juncos don't all look the same. In some areas the males have black heads, while in other areas the heads are dark gray or blue-gray. The colors of the back and sides vary from dark brown to bright cinnamon to pale pinkish brown. All are decidedly more colorful than the slate-colored juncos of the East.

Variations on a Theme

Although Oregon juncos are found throughout much of the West, four other junco varieties live there as well. All have separate breeding ranges in summer. But in winter, when they migrate farther south or to lower elevations in the mountains, they all may overlap.

The Black Hills area of South Dakota makes up most of the summer range of the white-winged junco. Despite its name, the bird has wings that are mostly gray with only two narrow white wing bars. Aside from those marks, it looks like a slightly larger, paler gray version of the slate-colored junco.

Just to the west, in Wyoming and southern Montana, is the summer range of juncos that are also large and pale, but with brown backs and pinkish buff sides. These are sometimes called pink-sided juncos but are occasionally considered a type of Oregon junco. Both white-winged and pink-sided juncos spread south in winter, mainly along the east side of the Rockies.

The mountains of Colorado, Utah and Nevada are the main summer range of the gray-headed junco. True to its name, this bird is mostly gray from head to tail, but the center of its back is a noticeably bright reddish brown. Like the other juncos, its bill is pale pink.

Just to the south, in the mountains of central Arizona and New Mexico, lives a bird that looks almost the same as the gray-headed junco but with a bill at least half black. Called the red-backed junco, it's less migratory than most of its cousins, generally staying in the same mountain forests during all seasons.

At some places in the West, three or four types of dark-eyed juncos may mix together in the same winter flocks. In the East, almost all the juncos are of the slate-colored type, but the occasional Oregon junco wanders as far east as the Atlantic Coast. Wherever they go, whether they herald the imminent coming of snow or just a mild change of seasons, these gentle, attractive birds are always welcome visitors.

Yellow-eyed junco

WHY DARK-EYED, ANYWAY?

In 1973, when species with names like slate-colored, Oregon and white-winged juncos were all combined into one species, scientists looked for a neutral name. They chose one to distinguish this bird from the yellow-eyed junco, a bird with bright yellow-orange eyes that lives mainly in the mountains of Mexico and southern Arizona.

White-winged junco

Red-backed junco

Gray-headed junco

Pink-sided junco

Birds After Dark

Unravel the mystery of what most birds do at night.

Eastern screech-owl

NOCTURNAL FLIERS SUCH AS whip-poor-wills and owls are just getting going when the sun sets. But what do birds that are active during the day do at night? Most will find a secluded spot to catch a coveted bit of shut-eye; however, sleep in the avian world is different than ours.

Birdy Catnaps

Instead of getting prolonged sleep, birds often take hundreds of short snoozes each day. In a variety of instances, birds are never really asleep—at least not in the way that people think. Half of a bird's brain stays active while it is resting, thanks to a phenomenon called unihemispheric slow-wave sleep. Remaining partially alert can help birds detect potential predators and deftly adjust to changing environmental conditions.

Some birds even nap while they fly. Magnificent frigatebirds, for example, sleep up to 12 hours per day when on land, but they are limited to less than an hour of rest

Young chickadee

per day when taking long cruises over the ocean, typically while they're riding warm air currents. Niels Rattenborg and colleagues report in *Nature Communications* that frigatebirds keep the eye that is connected to the awake and alert hemisphere of the brain facing the direction of flight. This gives a whole new meaning to thinking on the fly!

Built-In Blankets

Maintaining warmth is a challenge for sleeping birds. Feathers provide strong insulation, so birds tuck into themselves. As they snooze, ducks, geese and swans often bury their bills in their own feathers. Many species will also pull a leg up into their cozy feathered zones.

Birds rarely use nests as night roosts when they aren't actively incubating eggs or babies. Only a few cavity nesters like nuthatches, wrens and chickadees take to nest boxes throughout the year. Acorn woodpeckers, bluebirds, pygmy nuthatches and tree swallows have all been documented communally

American robin

roosting in small groups, each sharing the same cavities.

Perched for Shut-Eye

The vast majority of songbirds are natural perchers. This holds true even while they rest. Chalk it up to a bird's physique: To hold up its body weight, a bird will instinctively tighten its tendons and clamp its feet onto a branch.

Hummingbirds are the ultimate sleepers. Under extreme conditions, they've been found perched upside down, kind of like a bat. During cold

spells, hummingbirds lower their metabolism and body temperature and enter an overnight state called torpor, which almost mimics hibernation in other animals.

While they're dozing, it's not clear if birds dream, although they can experience bouts of rapid eye movement. Research in zebra finches has shown that brain neurons associated with song can be activated during sleep, yet this could simply be a way of reinforcing song learning instead of being proof of dreaming.

Wise Up on Owls

Nineteen spectacular species boast a toolbox of specialized traits and live in an array of environments, from thick woodlands to chilly tundra plains, in the United States and Canada. Here are some of the most fascinating facts about this one-of-a-kind group of birds.

WATCH OUT!
Owls aren't always apex predators. In fact, the top predator of this barred owl is the great horned owl.

Eastern
screech-owls

▲ **SURPRISING HUES**

Adult owls come in many colors. Even within a single species, they can be pale or dark or possibly sport different hues. It's most obvious in eastern screech-owls, which can have either mostly gray or mostly reddish-brown feathers.

Northern pygmy-owl

◀ GOOD MORNING

Some owls are actually early birds, rising to hunt initially at dawn and again at dusk. For example, great gray owls and northern pygmy-owls are active during the day when their preferred prey, small mammals and birds, are most prevalent.

◀ FANTASTIC FEET

Owls have surprisingly versatile feet. In fact, they're zygodactyl, meaning each foot has two toes pointing forward and two pointing backward. Even more impressive, one of the toes can swivel to help them perch or catch their prey.

◀ EYE WONDER

Owls' prominent yellow or dark eyes may seem round and nearly human, but their eyeballs are actually tube-shaped and cannot move in the sockets. Owls also have three different eyelids to keep those peepers healthy and clean.

Great horned owl

TURNING HEADS

To make up for their static eyes, owls are able to rotate their heads 270 degrees. They have twice as many vertebrae in their neck as humans do, along with special circulatory adaptations to allow blood flow to the head when it's fully turned.

Short-eared owl

Great gray owl

Great gray owl in a defensive posture

▲ ON ALERT

When an owl feels cornered or protective of its nest, the bird may make hissing noises, fluff its facial feathers, raise its wings and fan out its tail feathers.

▶ SIZING UP

Female owls tend to be larger than males in both wingspan and weight, although researchers are unsure why that's the case.

FAMOUS OWLS

Owls are beloved birds that have played a part in folklore and mythology, including that of the ancient Greeks. Athena, the goddess of wisdom, is often depicted with an owl. Today, they're fixtures of pop culture. Mr. Owl uses his smarts to find out how many licks it takes to get to the center of a Tootsie Pop, and Woodsy Owl offers the advice to never be a dirty bird and "Give a hoot, don't pollute."

Northern saw-whet owl

Great
horned
owl

▲ GIVE A HOOT

The great horned has the soft, deep call that many people associate with owls, but not every member of the family musters a traditional hoot. Northern saw-whets, for example, are named after their rather unusual call, which sounds like the process of sharpening a saw on a whetstone.

Snowy
owl

Burrowing owls spend most of their lives close to the ground, hunting and managing their nests.

▲ GOING LOW

Forget the treetops—burrowing owls live in underground dens in grasslands and deserts. They group together in colonies, often residing in the burrows left behind by animals such as prairie dogs, tortoises and skunks.

▶ TRAINED EARS

Many owls have asymmetrical ears, which helps them pinpoint the location of prey. Usually one ear is positioned higher or lower than the other, hidden underneath layers and layers of feathers. The two large feather tufts that long-eared owls sport at the top of their heads have nothing to do with their hearing; scientists believe they help the bird blend into its surrounding.

◀ SILENT GLIDES

Relative to the size of their bodies, owls have incredibly large wings that allow them to glide both slowly and silently. The structure of the feathers also diffuses some of the noise that flapping creates.

Long-eared owl

CHAPTER 5

Captured Beauty

Get inspired by nature photography taken by Birds & Blooms *readers.*

Motherly Love

Sweet moments between bird moms and their young come into focus.

WORKING HARD
Female eastern kingbirds take on almost all of the chick-feeding duties.

◄**We've been fortunate** enough to have a pair of eastern bluebirds raise a family in our yard. This picture from early spring shows the mama with the year's first set of fledglings. It was about two days after they had fledged, and it was time for chow! Mama had them all lined up, and each one wanted to be fed first. It was amazing to watch the family: the parents building the nest, the mama laying the eggs, and the chicks hatching and then flying out to start their own lives.

Karla Mayberry
CHESAPEAKE, VIRGINIA

► **It's always fun** and exciting to see birds, like this eastern kingbird, have a successful breeding season.

Dawn Denner
LEVITTOWN, PENNSYLVANIA

While walking the trails at the Mead Botanical Garden in Florida, I experienced this amazing moment. A pileated woodpecker mother was feeding her chicks, and it was such a magnificent wildlife surprise! I was so happy to witness and photograph it.

Gilberto Sanchez-Perez
ORLANDO, FLORIDA

▶ **I love when ruby-throated hummingbirds** visit. This sweet lady grabbed the nesting material we put out, and flew into our tree. I documented every day: nest building, eggs, chicks, feeding and fledging. I took this photo when the mom came to feed her chicks before they fledged.

Stephanie Cullinan
ST. LOUIS, MISSOURI

▼ **I knew this female common merganser** was nesting, so I waited for her to have her little ones. Once they were all in the water together, they gave me some wonderful photo opportunities. I had so much fun watching them learn how to dive for food. The mother was very protective, keeping all of them as close to her as she could.

Barbara Frankenfield
HILLSBOROUGH, NEW JERSEY

SINGLE MOMS
Only female ruby-throated hummingbirds take care of the chicks. The males don't play a role.

▲ **Being a parent** is a difficult job, especially when you're a killdeer and you nest in the open. I was very excited when I took this photo—truly amazed to have the opportunity to capture this image of a bird that both my spouse and I love. I've taken many pictures of killdeer in the past, but none quite as good as this one.

Emma Manuel
CALL, TEXAS

▶ **This mallard mother** decided to make her nest in the front garden of the bank where I work. We made sure she had enough food and water.

Isabel Fernald
VALDOSTA, GEORGIA

LATE BLOOMERS

Young sandhill cranes stay with their parents for about 10 months and follow them in migration.

One of the joys of living in Florida is the vast variety of interesting, beautiful birds. This particular crane and colt wandered by me on a trail at the Circle B Bar Reserve, just a 10-minute drive from my home. I sat down at the side of the trail when I noticed them coming, hoping they wouldn't let my presence stop them. They passed right by with barely a glimpse my way!

Melissa Hager
LAKELAND, FLORIDA

Bloom Tales

Every photograph tells a story in this collection of botanic adventures.

Cactuses bloom here in Arizona each spring, but this night-blooming Argentine giant I saw in Fountain Hills is pretty rare. The great majority of this species' blooms are white instead of pink. This particular bloom caught my eye one early morning as I was on my way to the store. I was very lucky because the flowers stay open for about six hours before wilting in the late morning. I quickly went home to grab my Nikon D750 and 50 mm lens. I got the shot I wanted!

Spencer Fairbanks
FOUNTAIN HILLS, ARIZONA

► **Being a birder,** I have feeders all over my yard. At times, unexpected plantings can pop up after birds drop morsels under feeders. This sunflower in the midst of roses was certainly a surprise. I just couldn't bring myself to pull it. The center's geometric patterns caught my attention and became my focus.

Stephanie Schick
HOUSTON, TEXAS

► **I took this image** of a blanket flower at the Inniswood Metro Garden in Westerville, Ohio, where I'm always on the lookout for hummingbirds, as well as butterflies and other insects. The colors of this bloom really set it apart. I hung the photo up and enjoy looking at it.

Richard Schnuerer
NEW ALBANY, OHIO

Driving on Highway 81 outside of Duncan, Oklahoma, my wife and I passed wildflowers growing in the median. I parked on the side of the highway, then walked over to the median and got down on my knees to take pictures of Indian paintbrushes and bluebonnets.

Ted Belling
YUKON, OKLAHOMA

In late spring of last year, a friend from a nearby town gave me this beautiful pink poppy. I placed a black poster board behind the flower and took this picture with a Nikon D750.

Tom Morack
COOKEVILLE, TENNESSEE

► I decided my portfolio was in need of a few good flower photos. With such a pretty moth orchid in full bloom right on my porch, the subject choice was easy. The plant was in a pot, so I moved it in front of some nice backyard greenery. This photo is special because the orchid was a gift for my wife. I was pleased with the results.

Tim Smith
NOKOMIS, FLORIDA

▼ Last year, I was taking some test shots with a new lens on a Nikon D500 and happened to stumble across this scene—a hydrangea with a bee. I didn't really think much of the shot at first, but during processing it came to life and now it's one of my favorites. Watching nature at work is amazing.

Lance Bruce
ZEBULON, NORTH CAROLINA

▲ I saw these water lilies in San Fransisco one summer. I like this shot because it shows some of the life stages of this beautiful flower. I used a Canon EOS 20D camera to take this photo, which is now one of my very favorites.

Leslie Howells
OXFORD, MARYLAND

► As a photographer for decades, I focus my time on the beauty provided by flowers. I've grown to especially love the purple passionflower for its unique features. My love grew immensely when I discovered this vine growing in the flower garden adjacent to an antique shop. I was able to capture this mature bloom along with a bud soon to open.

Joe Bob Hall
HOLLY LAKE RANCH, TEXAS

Persian shield plants have wonderful purple foliage that is quite striking. Recently, I've renewed my interest in nature and my passion for photography, which is how I learned about this plant. Aside from being outdoors more, I'm working in the backyard, growing my own wildlife-friendly habitat and pollinator garden, and contributing to various local arboretums and gardens as well as education programs.

Robert Blumenstock
WEST CALDWELL, NEW JERSEY

Hummingbird Love

Marvel at these small wonders in action—diving in for nectar, fluttering their wings and grabbing attention like no other.

I keep a bubbling jar fountain in the middle of my garden that attracts many different birds. Some of my favorite birds to watch splash around are hummingbirds. This young male Anna's hummingbird visited a few days in a row in June, each time inspecting the fountain a little bit closer. Finally, he decided to be brave and truly dive into the water. I was happy to catch him in action!

Jaklyn Larsen
FLORENCE, OREGON

▲ In late spring, I was lucky to find an Anna's hummingbird nest with two newly hatched babies. Over the course of about three weeks, I visited the nest often and documented the progress of the family with my camera. In this moment, Mama was just returning to her nest of two well-fed babies, both with beaks wide open in anticipation of their next meal.

Paul Marto
WEST JORDAN, UTAH

► I was weeding my garden when a broad-tailed hummingbird came to visit the flowers next to me. I usually have my camera with me, so I quickly grabbed it and snapped as many photos as I could before this little guy zipped away. The flier mostly stayed on the side where I couldn't see it, but for a few seconds it came perfectly into view.

Sonja Puhek
COLORADO SPRINGS, COLORADO

This juvenile male ruby-throated hummingbird kept coming back to this rose of Sharon bud to rest briefly. After a few attempts, I finally got an image with his tongue, which appeared for a split second. He seemed quite comfortable in my presence.

Vanessa Woodlock
GOLDSBORO, NORTH CAROLINA

The Calliope is a rare summer migrant to the urban areas of San Diego. When a male was spotted close to where I live, I went repeatedly to the area of the sighting to perform a stakeout. I finally got a glimpse of this beautiful hummingbird just long enough to snap a couple of photos as it visited white sage flowers. It's the only Calliope I've ever seen.

Aicha Ennaciri
SAN DIEGO, CALIFORNIA

► This male Anna's appeared in my backyard in Southern California. He has many perching spots in my yard, but he came out to guard the top of the hedges this day. I used a Canon EOS 6D Mark II camera.

Monica Slack
EL CAJON, CALIFORNIA

▼ I captured this wonderful image of a ruby-throated hummingbird while at the Stony Creek Metropark Nature Center in Shelby Township, Michigan. The experience inspired my family and me to grow a fairly large patch of scarlet bee balm in our hummingbird garden.

Sharon Sauriol
WASHINGTON, MICHIGAN

▲ **Shortly after** hanging our flag on our deck, this male ruby-throated hummingbird flew in front of it to the feeder. The sight of it captured my patriotic heart, so I ran for my camera to take a quick photo of two of my favorite things together: our flag waving in the breeze and a lovely hummingbird in flight.

Barbara Reams
PINCKNEY, MICHIGAN

▶ **Each August** we stay with our friend in Bethany Beach, Delaware, to photograph hummers. We had hoped that the fast fliers would go for her hibiscus flowers, but the whole time we were there, no dice. I started to pack up my camera equipment to leave when this ruby-throated showed up!

Suzanne Cassidy
HUGHESVILLE, MARYLAND

ALLEN'S OR RUFOUS?
Could be either! Female and immature birds of the two species are almost identical. They mainly differ in the shapes of certain tail feathers, which aren't visible in this photo.

This precious jewel of nature was ready to take a bath. I took this photo in the early morning, not during the high heat of the day. Hummingbirds like to clean their bills from all that sticky nectar and pollen and also wash off their delicate feathers to keep fresh and clean.

Gilberto Sanchez
ORLANDO, FLORIDA

My husband hangs several hummingbird feeders every year from a long wire across our deck. For this photo I was using a new Canon telephoto lens on my camera, which was mounted on a tripod. Hoping to get a good shot of a male ruby-throated who had his wings out, just daring another hummer to come close, I snapped a series of photos to get this particular one.

Felice Bond
WILLIAMSBURG, VIRGINIA

► **This female black-chinned hummingbird** was attempting to drink sugar water from the feeder in our front yard when a wasp decided it also wanted some. The photo shows anxiety and frustration coming from both the bird and the wasp as they attempted to use the sugar-water feeder at the same time.

Ginny Phillips
PRESCOTT, ARIZONA

▼ **Cardinal flowers rely** heavily on ruby-throated hummingbirds for pollination. As the bird's forehead comes in contact with a bloom, it collects pollen, which the hummingbird then hopefully carries over to another cardinal flower bloom.

Laurie Dirkx
ONTARIO, NEW YORK

The Allure of Moths

Up-close photos of these day-flying insects prove they're not all elusive creatures of the night.

I saw this beautiful cecropia moth at my neighbor's place. It had recently emerged and wasn't able to fly right away, so it was easy for me to quickly snap a photo.

Brenda Doherty
ARISS, ONTARIO

My son and my granddaughter Morgan visited me one spring. While playing in the yard, Morgan spotted a "big butterfly lying on the flowers." It was actually a polyphemus moth that had just emerged from its cocoon and was drying itself. Talk about perfect timing! If it had been only a few minutes later, we might have missed this. Its coloring was so perfect. Wow!

Cherie Heitman
SEDALIA, MISSOURI

►While hiking the trails in Vermilion Provincial Park here in Vermilion, Alberta, I spotted this Virginia ctenucha moth. I saw it three days straight before it stayed still long enough for me to capture a photo with my iPhone.

Ruth Avramovic
VERMILION, ALBERTA

▼The white-lined sphinx moth is often referred to as a hummingbird moth—they do get mistaken for hummingbirds! These moths love the zinnias that bloom from summer into fall in my garden.

Marina Schultz
FRUITA, COLORADO

▲ I was attempting to capture a close-up of what I thought was a bumblebee on the banks of Polecat Creek in Randleman, North Carolina, but further inspection revealed that it was an eight-spotted forester moth. It was wonderful to catch a glimpse of this elusive moth sipping nectar from a beautiful dogwood, and to watch this pollinator doing nature's work.

Patricia Wells
YORKTOWN, VIRGINIA

▶ While pulled over at a rest stop at the Pennsylvania-West Virginia border, I was thrilled to see this imperial moth perfectly framed on a glass brick in the wall of the visitor center. What a most surprising welcome to wild and wonderful West Virginia!

April Livingston
MOBILE, ALABAMA

High in the mountains of Flagstaff, Arizona, the groves of wildflowers and aspen trees bring the wild *Gnophaela discreta* (a moth without a common name) by the hundreds. Often you'll see several at one time on a single flower.

Kerysa Ford
PHOENIX, ARIZONA

After direct sowing
milkweed seeds one fall, I was pleased to see that they grew into a healthy patch the following summer. I spied this showy specimen—a milkweed tiger moth caterpillar—while looking for evidence of monarch activity, and I was happy to learn that milkweed hosts this species as well! I'm so glad I got this snapshot, because it was the only time I spotted this caterpillar.

Elizabeth Griswold
MADISON, CONNECTICUT

What's your best hummingbird photography tip?

The shutterbugs of our *Birds & Blooms* community share their best advice for taking pictures of these speedy birds.

Anna's hummingbird

Sit and watch the hummers. They'll get used to you being there. Then you can sit all day snapping away to your heart's content.

Jackie Taylor HUBERT, NORTH CAROLINA

I set my camera up on a tripod a few feet from my feeder. I focus the shot, attach a remote control shutter, then have a seat. Rather than watching the feeder through the viewfinder the whole time, I listen for the noise made by the birds' wings.

Billy Walker FORT WALTON BEACH, FLORIDA

Wear red! Hummingbirds are really drawn to the color, whether it's on a flower or you're wearing it yourself. I carry a red umbrella to stay out of the sun, wear my brightest red shirt and sit in front of my zinnia garden with my camera at the ready.

Mary Sullivan DELANO, MINNESOTA

I put out feeders with perches on them. The birds stop long enough for me to snap a picture.

Mary Clark MANTACHIE, MISSISSIPPI

Patience. Lots and lots of patience.

Susan Chilkotowsky-Kain MARLTON, NEW JERSEY

Ruby-throated hummingbird at pink salvia

Open your camera's aperture all the way and focus manually while you take dozens of photos.

Vincent Drexler CANAL FULTON, OHIO

CHAPTER 6

Garden Know-How

Get plant and flower savvy with our down-to-earth advice.

COMPOST
CLUE
Turn compost
piles regularly
to introduce
enough oxygen
and prevent a
strong smell.

Garden Myths Debunked!

A lot of fantastic gardening advice has been shared through the generations, but some erroneous recommendations have trickled down as well. Here are some myths that can be officially laid to rest.

Compost piles smell awful.

Fact: If your compost pile has anything but a pleasant earthy smell, it's not being properly worked. If there is a lack of oxygen in the pile, your compost will still break down—slowly—by an anaerobic process, but it will have a swampy smell. To help mitigate any odor, turn the pile regularly to introduce oxygen to the mix. Add some dry leaves and a few shovelfuls of soil to keep materials from turning slimy.

You need to water plants daily.

Fact: Container plants may need a dousing daily, but those in landscapes do not. It's better to water your garden once or twice a week and to irrigate deeply. Shallow watering encourages roots to stay near the surface. Instead, you want the roots to grow deep so plants are self-sufficient during dry periods. Obviously, cactuses and succulents need less water. Check the soil moisture before getting out the hose.

You should paint tree wounds after pruning.

Fact: This is an old practice of tree care that has fallen out of favor. In most cases, painting a blemish doesn't serve a purpose and could actually have a negative impact on the sealing of the wound. However, there are exceptions: Tree-wound paint can help if you are pruning a tree that could be threatened by the disease-carrying beetles attracted to a fresh wound, such as sap or bark beetles . In particular, consider it for the types of oaks that are susceptible to oak wilt.

To ripen green tomatoes, set them on a sunny windowsill.

Fact: Sunlight is not needed. For slow ripening, put tomatoes in a cool basement and wrap them individually in newspaper. This helps contain the ethylene gas given off by the fruit, which stimulates ripening. Store your ripe and unripe fruits together for faster results.

Leaving grass clippings on the lawn will cause thatch to build up.

Fact: Short grass clippings do not contribute to thatch—a thick layer of dead plant debris that makes it difficult for new turf to emerge. In fact, it's advised to leave your grass clippings in place rather than bagging them, especially if you have a mulching mower. It's less work, and the clippings are a free source of nitrogen for your lawn. For the best-looking grass, always keep your lawn mower blades sharp.

Wood chips always make the best mulch.

Fact: That depends on where you're using them. Wood chips are a wonderful mulch for a natural garden, but they hold too much moisture for cactuses and succulents. There are other caveats, too. Mainly, don't spread them too heavily (no more than 3 inches thick) and don't pile them against plant stems—this is known to cause problems with bugs and rot.

Newspaper and cardboard are superb weed barriers.

Fact: In certain situations, these materials can be used as weed barriers and then covered with wood chips or organic mulch. The problem is, they can impede water penetration and gas exchange if they become too wet or too dry. The same goes if they're applied too heavily. Use no more than four to six sheets of newspaper or one layer of cardboard as sheet mulch.

You can't grow anything near a black walnut tree.

Fact: While black walnut trees do release an allelopathic chemical called juglone, which can inhibit the growth of some plants, many others are able to grow beneath and near them. Zinnias, daylilies, Shasta daisies, begonias, Japanese maples, purple coneflowers, phlox and forsythias are capable of thriving nearby. Your local cooperative extension or master gardener program will have a complete list for your region.

The reason pepper plants aren't setting fruit is because the soil is too rich.

Fact: While overly rich soil will favor foliage over flowers, it won't stop pepper plants from bearing fruit altogether. It's more likely that a lack of flowering (and subsequent pepper production) is due to weather. A hot, drying wind will cause flowers to drop off. Also, many pepper plants are very temperature sensitive; flowers will drop off below 55 degrees or above 85 degrees.

For the best garden soil, be sure to cultivate regularly.

Fact: Some cultivation is helpful with heavy or compacted soils, but too much can turn the topsoil into a powdery dust that repels water and is not conducive to root growth. Also, frequent cultivation exposes more of the soil to the sun, which can dry it out and cut down the amount of its beneficial microbes.

Houseplant Rescue

You've got common indoor plant problems—and we've got answers.

THE FIRST STEP in treating your indoor plants is to understand the likely dilemmas and their solutions. Here are a few common questions that come up about ailing houseplants and how to address them. Once you know what to look for, you'll be surprised by how quickly your diagnostic skills improve.

Golden pothos

Why Are the Leaves Yellow?

Start by evaluating your watering habits. Watering too frequently or infrequently can cause leaves to yellow. Tropical plants prefer moist soil, while cactuses and succulents like the soil to go dry between watering. Always use your finger to check the top 1 to 2 inches of soil for moisture before watering.

Increase success by using containers with drainage holes, or use self-watering pots with "weep holes" that allow excess water to escape. Pour off any water that collects in the saucer to avoid root rot. Or place pebbles in the saucer to elevate the pot above the excess water.

Once you rule out improper watering, it's time to review your fertilization schedule. Let the plants be your guide. Pale, yellow or stunted leaves may mean the plants need a nutrient boost. Use a diluted solution of houseplant fertilizer and only fertilize actively growing plants from spring through early fall, even if they're always indoors.

Additionally, mites, aphids and scale pests can suck plant juices, causing the leaves to turn yellow or brown. A strong blast of water dislodges many of these insects. A couple of applications of insecticidal soap, too, will help manage these pests and even immature scale insects. Organic horticulture oil labeled for use on houseplants is effective at controlling pests at all stages.

What Do Brown Edges Mean?

If your plant is sporting crispy, dark edges, it may mean you need to water more often. Check the soil moisture and slowly reduce the number of days between waterings. Watch your plants for signs of improvement.

Lack of humidity could also be the cause. Tropical plants prefer higher humidity than

Snake plant

Chinese evergreen

Cast iron plant

Philodendron

we have in our homes. When we turn on the heat in winter, there's even less moisture in the air. One solution is to group plants together. That way, as one loses moisture through its leaves, its close neighbors benefit. You can also place plants on saucers or trays filled with pebbles and water. Set a pot on the pebbles above the water. As water evaporates, it increases the humidity around the plant, where it is needed.

Why Is My Plant So Spindly?

Uneven or insufficient light is likely the cause of these problems. Give plants a quarter-turn every few weeks to promote balanced growth. Let in more light if plants have thin stems and excessive space between each set of leaves.

Plants that need a lot of light can thrive when placed in front of an east- or west-facing window. Place low-light plants 6 feet back and off to the side of these windows or near a north-facing one. Once you provide the right amount of light, pinch off the growing tips of leggy plants to encourage compact growth.

What Are These Dark Spots?

Brown, black and water-soaked spots on leaves and stems often indicate that a fungal or bacterial disease is the problem.

Adjust the watering schedule and do not allow plants to sit in excess water. Often that alone is enough to stop the disease's progress. Remove and dispose of any soft, discolored stems and leaves. Trim off any rotten roots and repot in fresh potting mix in a container slightly larger than the remaining roots.

Why Are the New Leaves Small?

When new leaves are smaller than normal, it could be because the plant is pot-bound. Or, it may need to be fertilized or moved to a brighter location. Keep an eye out for other clues when making your diagnosis.

If water runs out of the pot quickly and roots are filling the container, it's time to move your plant to the next size of container. Avoid moving pot-bound plants to much larger containers, which can slow above-ground growth and lead to root rot. If the pot size seems adequate, evaluate your fertilizer schedule and light.

What's the Sticky Stuff?

Pests such as mites, aphids, scale bugs and mealybugs drink up plant juices, secreting the excess. This clear sticky substance is called honeydew and is often the first clue these pests are feeding on your plants. As described earlier, try rinsing off the bugs first. If that doesn't get rid of them, move on to insecticidal soap or organic horticulture oil labeled for houseplants.

Can I Get Rid of Small Flies?

Fungus gnats are not harmful but certainly are annoying. The immature gnats feed on organic matter in the soil while the adult flies flit around your home.

To evict them, allow the soil to go a bit drier and trap the adults with a container of apple cider vinegar on the countertop. You could also use organic *Bacillus thuringiensis israelensis*, which is in Mosquito Bits. Sprinkle the product over the surface of the soil and repeat as often as the label directions recommend.

TOUGH AS NAILS
Match these plants with the right amount of sun and water to expect success.

- Snake plant (*Sanseveria* spp.)
- Philodendron
- Pothos
- Chinese evergreen
- Cast iron plant
- ZZ plant

ZZ plant

One-Pot Wonders

These plants don't need a partner—they shine on their own.

1

TRIM TIME
Keep *brachyscomes* looking their best by shearing them back once the blooms start to fade.

1. Brasco Violet brachyscome

BRACHYSCOME 'DBRASC9', ANNUAL

This long bloomer sticks around all the way from spring until frost. It features violet blossoms that resemble daisies with their golden centers. The plant's mounded habit is 12 to 18 inches tall with a slightly smaller width.

Why we love it: Not fussy at all, this plant is both low maintenance and heat tolerant.

2. Senorita Rosalita spider flower

CLEOME 'INNCLEOSR'
ZONES 10 TO 11 OR ANNUAL

A container-friendly, shorter version of an old cottage favorite, this cleome has bright blooms without the thorns or self-seeding tendencies of the species. It grows 2 to 4 feet tall and tends to thrive under full sun.

Why we love it: The uniquely shaped and colored flowers decorate the entire stem.

3. Wave petunia

PETUNIA X HYBRIDA, ANNUAL

As the name suggests, these petunias feature a wave of vibrant color. Growing just 5 to 7 inches tall but spreading 2 to 4 feet, Wave petunias can engulf a container and bloom from spring until frost.

Why we love it: Not only does it offer nonstop flowers in many colors, but it's also known to tolerate high heat and humidity.

4. Superbells calibrachoa

CALIBRACHOA HYBRID,
ZONES 9 TO 11 OR ANNUAL

With its notable heat tolerance and continuous bloom, Superbells is a big-time favorite with container gardeners. Just 6 to 12 inches tall with a spread twice as wide, this appealing species comes in dozens of colors and is known to attract thirsty hummingbirds.

Why we love it: Deadheading is not needed—this variety offers flowers all summer long.

5. Heart to Heart caladium

CALADIUM HORTULANUM 'FLATTER ME',
ZONES 10 TO 11 OR ANNUAL

You won't mind the lack of flowers with leaves like this. The flashy leaf pattern features a mottled mix of light and dark green with striking hot pink veins. Flatter Me reaches 15 to 20 inches tall and 10 to 14 inches wide. It can thrive in pots.
Why we love it: Use it to brighten up a shady outdoor spot or as a houseplant.

6. Petite Knock Out rose

ROSA 'MEIBENBINO', ZONES 5 TO 10

The same flower power of the standard Knock Out rose is now in a compact size, perfect for containers. The red blooms are abundant on this bushy variety that grows 18 inches tall.
Why we love it: There's a lot to like when it comes to the long-lasting blooms and nonfading bright red color.

7. Compact Tropical Rose SunPatiens

IMPATIENS X HYBRIDA 'SAKIMP037',
ZONES 10 TO 11 OR ANNUAL

The vibrant reddish pink flowers are hard to miss, but the two-tone green and cream foliage also draws plenty of attention. This colorful impatiens reaches about 2 feet tall and 14 to 20 inches wide.
Why we love it: The bright, fun variegation provides an additional visual spark. Plus, the plant has the ability to grow in sun to part shade.

8. Autumn Starburst dwarf azalea

RHODODENDRON 'ROBLEZE', ZONES 6 TO 10

Go ahead, put a shrub in a pot! This dwarf azalea reaches a height of 3 to 5 feet and has a slightly wider spread. The eye-catching flowers are red and pink, and at 2½ inches across, they're hard to miss.

Why we love it: The spring coloring is simply stunning, and it reblooms later in the season.

9. Purple Potion trailing lantana

LANTANA SELLOWIANA 'MONPUR', ZONES 9 TO 11 OR ANNUAL

With a form perfectly suited to containers, this trailer grows just 8 to 12 inches tall but splays out 3 to 6 feet. As a bonus, its violet blooms keep the boisterous plant company all summer long. Research this species before planting, as it can be invasive in some areas.

Why we love it: Plant one in a container and another at the base of the pot for a two-tiered treat.

10. Oo-La-La bougainvillea

BOUGAINVILLEA 'MONKA', ZONES 10 TO 11 OR ANNUAL

This vine grows just 1½ feet tall but can spread 6 to 8 feet to fill a container with its tropical color. It's practically drenched in magenta bracts, which are modified leaves surrounding the actual white flowers that attract pollinators.

Why we love it: The compact form is great for hanging baskets, and the bracts last longer than other types of bougainvillea.

Be the Best Plant Parent

Grow (or refresh) your green thumb knowledge by diving into these essential tasks.

TAKING CARE OF PLANTS in a garden is kind of like raising kids. You've got to feed them, keep them safe and give them plenty of room to grow! Here are the most important responsibilities every plant owner needs to be aware of, along with advice on how to correctly accomplish these tasks, whether you're a proud new parent or a seasoned pro.

Watering

While watering is important (and fun—who doesn't love spraying the garden hose?), be careful not to overdo it. Believe it or not, overwatering is just as much of a problem as underwatering. Some plants in pots need daily drinks, while others in the garden prefer their soil to dry out completely before another shower. Look to the leaves for cues. If they are yellow or brown (and drooping) even though the soil is wet, that's a sign that they're probably getting too much moisture. It's better to water deeply than frequently. Sprinkle water at the plant's base, directing the moisture down to the roots where it does the most good.

Fertilizing

Just like humans, plants can't live on sun alone. Rich topsoil with lots of compost will provide a lot of what your hungry little green friends need, but occasionally you'll want to give them an extra boost. Plants need nitrogen, phosphorus and potassium, and most will thrive on a general fertilizer. But, as with water, you can definitely have too much of a good thing. Overfertilizing contaminates groundwater and harms plants, so follow the directions and feed only when it's really needed.

Weeding

Experienced gardeners will tell you that it's easy to identify weeds: They're the ones that grow twice as fast and three times as big as the plants that are supposed to be thriving in the same place! Weeding is one of those chores you've simply got to face. Weeds aren't only unsightly; they're also greedy. They take nutrients and water from the soil that your precious plants desperately need. Grab invaders at the base and do your best to pull them out, root and all. Otherwise, they'll be sprouting back before you even have a chance to clean the dirt from under your fingernails.

Mulching

Think of mulch like a babysitter that is helping protect your plants when you're not there. Mulch helps soil retain moisture and suppress weeds. It also keeps roots cool during hot summer days and keeps them warm when the temps drop. Mulch comes in lots of different types, including shredded wood, evergreen needles and hay. The bigger nuggets take longer to break down, meaning they'll last longer. Whichever you

choose, add a fresh layer of 2 to 4 inches each spring (a 4-inch layer of mulch is best for preventing weeds), and pull it back slightly to keep it from brushing up against the plant stems and tree trunks.

Pruning

The best plant parents know that kids need some discipline. Pruning keeps shrubs and trees in check, helping them grow full and healthy. Timing is key. Many shrubs set their flower buds weeks or months before bloom, so if you prune at the wrong time, you lose all those beauties. Prune spring flowering shrubs after they finish blooming and summer bloomers in

late winter or early spring. Use loppers with sharp blades, making cuts at a 45-degree angle, above an outward-facing bud or fork.

Controlling Pests

Nothing is more annoying to a gardener than finding holes chewed in leaves, or aphids sucking the life out of buds. Resist the urge to go straight to pesticides, though, since these can harm pollinators and other beneficial bugs. Start by removing the pests by hand or with a strong blast from the hose. If they return, identify the pest and select the most eco-friendly option to remove them, such as an insecticidal soap or horticultural oil (be careful to follow label instructions).

Remember: Treat pests as they appear rather than spraying wholesale for problems you may not even have.

Deadheading and Pinching

Flowering plants put all their energy into first producing blooms, then turning those into seeds. After all, that's how plants make more plants! If you want to encourage more blooms instead of seeds on reflowering plants, pinch or snip off dead flower heads. For a fuller and more bushy appearance, pinch off new growth just above a leaf node or bud. This actually encourages the plant to grow two new stems where there once was only one.

Make Snails Slink Away

Try seven nontoxic ways to keep slugs and snails from running roughshod over your garden.

Plants with stiff leaves, such as geraniums, tend to resist snails.

YOU MAY NOT SEE THEM OFTEN, but slugs and snails make their presence known in a garden. Eating up to six times their weight in plant material per night, these mollusks can leave plants looking like Swiss cheese. Although they're most active in the evening, it is possible to combat the pests any time of day with these surprisingly simple strategies.

1. Use Beer as Bait

Bury tuna cans or plastic yogurt cups in the dirt up to their rims, then crack a beer and fill the containers (the older and more stale the beer, the better). Both slugs and snails will be attracted to the yeasty aroma, then fall in and drown. Replace the beer as needed.

2. Find an Edge

Add an inch of coarse sand, diatomaceous earth (look for it online or at garden centers), or eggshells in a 3-inch-wide band around plants. In dry weather, the slimy creatures won't cross over the sharp material to get to their buffet.

3. Repurpose Ashes

Slugs and snails avoid wood ashes because of their alkalinity. In the garden, distribute wood ashes from your fireplace (but not charcoal, which may contain chemicals). Over time, ashes can increase the pH of soil, so use sparingly.

4. Band Together

It's not cost effective for a large number of plants, but place copper bands around prized plants that are vulnerable to attack. When slugs slither across the copper bands, the moisture in their slimy trails sets off an electrical shock, keeping the pests from continuing their journeys up the stem.

Japanese beetle on St. John's wort

5. Shop Smart

Choose your baits wisely. Those including iron phosphate are considered safe for other animals but deadly for slugs and snails. The pests will eat the bait, stop feeding and die within a few days. According to the Oregon State University Extension, iron-phosphate baits are just as effective as metaldehyde baits but are not toxic to wildlife or pets. If you're shopping, look for brand names like Sluggo or Garden Safe Slug & Snail Bait.

6. Go on the Hunt

Sundown is the best time to sneak around. Use a flashlight to hunt for snails and slugs in the evening, about two hours after sunset. If you're searching during the day, look for the pests in shady, damp areas and beneath leaves and garden debris. When you find a slug or snail, shake some salt on it. Surprisingly, salt is deadly to snails and slugs, as it dehydrates them. Or pick up the pest and place it in a jar filled with soapy water.

7. Lure and Eliminate

Set a trap by placing some boards in shady areas of the garden where slugs and snails hide in the daytime. Then simply lift up the boards and scrape off the pests. You can do the same thing with inverted grapefruit rinds, especially in smaller spaces. Turn the rinds over in the morning, scrape out the pests and destroy them. And enjoy your pesticide-free garden with fewer slugs.

PLAN TO BE PEST FREE

Use these simple techniques to keep your yard safe from bad bugs, as well as from harmful pesticides.

BLAST THEM. Dislodge both aphids and mites with a blast from the hose.

LATHER UP. Shake adult Japanese beetles off plants and into a soapy jar of water.

REMOVE IT. Other than small-scale infestations, it's usually easiest to destroy the plant.

WELCOME PREDATORS. Encourage lady beetles to visit and eat aphids and spider mites.

PICK 'EM. Remove larger pests such as squash bugs and tomato hornworms from plants and dispose of them.

Hornworm on a tomato

Early Risers

Fill your garden with the very first flowers that bloom in the spring.

1

1. Reticulated iris

IRIS RETICULATA, ZONES 5 TO 9

Unlike other irises that stretch tall toward the sky, the reticulated iris grows only a few inches high. When massed together, these abundant and showy blossoms put on quite the amazing early spring display. **Why we love it:** This is a deer-resistant bulb that flaunts deep cobalt blue petals offset by yellow markings. It makes an especially striking statement when mixed with snowdrops and crocuses.

2. Bloodroot

SANGUINARIA CANADENSIS, ZONES 3 TO 8

Always a welcome sign that warmer weather is on the way, these large, short-lasting white flowers have yellow centers. The flowers grow from a rhizome. Single stems with one leaf and flower emerge from the structure, slowly growing into a larger clump. **Why we love it:** Bloodroot craves spring sun and summer shade, so it's a perfect pick for a woodland garden under deciduous trees.

3. Forsythia

FORSYTHIA SPP., ZONES 4 TO 8

Cheery yellow flowers along graceful bending branches are a welcome match for spring sunshine. Bees and butterflies zero in on this early nectar source, which blooms best in full sun but can tolerate some shade. **Why we love it:** Ranging from 2-foot dwarf varieties to those reaching 10 feet high and wide, forsythia shrubs fit in almost any garden space.

4. Siberian squill

SCILLA SIBERICA, ZONES 2 TO 8

Brilliant blue blooms adorn this low-growing squill, which spreads freely to quickly colonize an area. Due to its invasive tendencies, do not plant it in or near a natural wooded area. **Why we love it:** This incredibly hardy stalwart is resistant to deer, rabbits and chipmunks. Mix traditional blue squill with white Alba squill for a spectacular show.

5

5. Witch hazel

HAMAMELIS JAPONICA, ZONES 5 TO 8

American witch hazel (*H. virginiana*) is one of the few plants that blooms in the fall, and the related Japanese witch hazel (*H. japonica*) takes over in late winter and early spring.

Why we love it: Witch hazel shrubs show off when other plants are sleeping. Try a golden combination of American and Japanese varieties.

6

6. Dutchman's breeches

DICENTRA CUCULLARIA, ZONES 3 TO 7

This beautiful but short-lasting woodland wildflower is gone by summer, along with its foliage. For a few weeks in spring, though, the delicate flowers hanging off their arching stems are a pure delight.

Why we love it: This relative of bleeding heart (*Lamprocapnos spectabilis*) is a classic that's ready to make a comeback in moist, well-draining gardens.

7

7. Celandine poppy

STYLOPHORUM DIPHYLLUM, ZONES 4 TO 9

It's always a welcome sight when this wildflower pops up. Celandine, native to the eastern U.S., enjoys rich, wet soil and an abundance of shade. Try to grow it under trees, where it naturalizes by self-seeding over time.

Why we love it: Flashes of yellow poppies, which spring forth from fuzzy buds, draw attention to shady spots in the garden. The large-lobed foliage is attractive, too.

8. Lenten rose

HELLEBORUS X HYBRIDUS, ZONES 4 TO 9

This sweet simple-care favorite is perfect for the shadier spaces in your garden. Over time, this prolific self-seeder colonizes an area. Its robust evergreen foliage is a crowd-pleaser all year long.

Why we love it: It's easy to want Lenten rose in all its striking colors: the almost black Midnight Ruffles, the burgundy-spotted pale petals of Rio Carnival and everything in between.

9. Flowering quince

CHAENOMELES SPECIOSA, ZONES 4 TO 8

This thorny shrub is an excellent low-maintenance border option. Plant it in full sun to ensure bountiful blossoms as winter gives way to warmer days. Quince tends to flower on old growth, so prune it in spring after it finishes blooming, if needed.

Why we love it: The red, pink or white flowers are followed by small hard yellow-green fruits that make delicious preserves and jellies.

10. Pasque flower

PULSATILLA SPP., ZONES 4 TO 8

The showy European pasque flower (*P. vulgaris*) usually boasts pale to deep purple petals, but red and white varieties are also available. The yellow centers draw the first pollinators of the season. *P. patens* is an American native found across the U.S., with blue-violet flowers.

Why we love it: This rabbit-resistant charmer puts on one of the earliest shows in spring. The blooms are followed by attractive fuzzy seed heads that have a beauty all their own.

Good-Lookin' Grass

Follow a few simple steps to keep ornamental varieties looking great well into autumn.

Use two large garden forks to easily divide grasses.

WHEN YOU THINK ABOUT GRASS, mowing, watering and fertilizing may come to mind. But those tasks apply just to lawns. When you consider ornamental grass, the maintenance is far less intensive. Still, you can take actions to make sure your ornamental grasses sail into fall and make it through winter looking sharp.

"Many homeowners like ornamental grasses because they are drought tolerant and rarely bothered by pests," says Iowa landscape designer Dori Hein. "They seldom need fertilizing, either. Fertilizing ornamental grasses may actually cause them to flop over."

But don't turn a blind eye—low maintenance doesn't equate to no maintenance. "Summer is the best time to keep an eye on watering needs, especially during the plant's first year while it's establishing roots," Dori says. "I like to put down a natural mulch, too, because it

Chameleon little bluestem

Aureola Hakone grass is attractive because it's low maintenance and it grows well in shade.

mimics natural conditions and feeds the plants as it breaks down. Just don't put the mulch up against the plant's base, because it can cause the crown to rot."

Once established, ornamental grasses have very few needs. "The big thing with grasses is cutting them back once a year and dividing them once every four or five years," Dori says.

Most gardeners leave their grasses in place for winter interest and to provide food for birds, cutting the grasses back to within a few inches of the ground in late winter or early spring.

"Cut back before the new shoots grow up through the old," Dori says, "or you'll wind up cutting off the new growth, too." In areas where wildfires are a seasonal concern, cut back grasses in fall to lessen the threat of fire.

You'll know it's time to divide grasses when a ring of living grass surrounds a dead center. "It's easier to divide most grasses when they are still short from their post-winter haircut so there's no foliage to get in the way," Dori says.

Late winter to early spring is also the best time to divide grasses that flower in late summer and fall. Use a sharp spade or root saw and separate the living portion of the grass into smaller sections a little bit bigger than a softball. Replant the sections, water well and enjoy through the seasons.

GROW MORE GRASS

Don't miss out on these five ornamental grass perks.

1. Screen unsightly utilities and other items around the yard.
2. Add some privacy by rimming the edge of a patio with tall ornamental grasses.
3. Soften the look of a structure, fence or corner.
4. Create a stage for other plants to pop against the grassy backdrop.
5. Offer ambiance with the relaxing sights and sounds of grasses swaying in the wind.

At-Home Harvest

A step-by-step guide to growing the best backyard pumpkins and gourds.

WHETHER THEY'RE DRESSING UP indoor and outdoor spaces in fall or starring in seasonal desserts, pumpkins and gourds are autumn musts. To harvest them from your own garden next year, follow these simple tips to get a head start on your personal patch.

Pumpkins and gourds are members of the *Cucurbitaceae* family. When growing your own, pick from the wide assortment available in seed catalogs or online. Certain pumpkins are best for carving, while others make the sweetest pies. Read carefully to select pumpkins that meet your garden goals. Fruit sizes range from mini to massive; colors include classic orange as well as white, red, green, blue and yellow; and shapes vary from flat to round to tall.

Gourds, too, are rewarding to grow yourself. Two main types are available to gardeners: hard-shell and ornamental. Hard-shell gourds, such as birdhouse or dipper gourds, can be dried and kept indefinitely. The fruits are also edible when harvested immature. Ornamental gourds produce unique fruits in a wide mix of shapes, sizes and colors. But these gourds aren't edible and don't dry well, so they're best used as decor in autumn and then added to the compost pile.

Perfect Planting

Though they are pretty easy to grow, success with pumpkins and gourds begins with selecting the right spot. They need at least eight hours of sun each day as well as room for the vines to roam. If you lack growing space, plant bush or semi-bush options that don't produce long vines.

Pumpkins and gourds are greedy plants, growing best when the soil is enhanced with several inches of compost or aged manure.

It's also a good idea to apply a slow-release organic vegetable fertilizer to the garden bed before doing any planting.

The heat-loving fruits shouldn't be rushed into the spring garden, since the seeds don't germinate well in cold soil. Wait until the soil has warmed to 70 degrees and your area's last frost date has passed. Then sow seeds or transplant seedlings into raised beds, in-ground gardens, straw bales, or hills, which are small mounds of soil piled up to improve drainage and raise soil temperature. Sow seeds ½ inch to 1 inch deep. Spacing depends on the selected variety, so refer to your seed packets for specific spacing information.

Taking Care

Once in the garden, pumpkins and gourds are easygoing. Keep an eye on soil moisture, watering deeply when the soil is dry. Water the soil, not the plant, as splashing water can increase the risk of soil-borne disease. Promote healthy growth by fertilizing every two to three weeks with either a liquid kelp or fish fertilizer.

Also watch out for pests like squash bugs and squash vine borers. If borers are an annual issue in your garden, wrap a 6-inch piece of aluminum foil around the base of each plant. This helps reduce the number of female vine borers laying eggs on the plant stems.

When several pumpkins have formed on each vine, pinch back the growing tip. This directs the plant's energy into maturing existing fruits rather than producing more flowers. The late flowers won't have time to mature into good-sized pumpkins. Pinching also leads to bigger pumpkins. Pinching hard-shell gourds is helpful too, but bear in mind: There's really no need to prune back the plants of ornamental gourds.

Harvesting

First-time growers may have a hard time knowing when it's time to harvest their pumpkins and gourds. The biggest clue is color. With a sharp pair of pruners, clip fruits from vines when they've turned their mature color. Leave a stem about 2 to 4 inches long attached to each fruit. Also, be sure to harvest before a hard frost hits, which can damage the fruits.

Let pumpkins and gourds cure in the sun for five to seven days if the weather allows. Curing keeps pumpkins from decaying too quickly. If cold and frost are threats, bring the fruits indoors to a warm spot with decent air circulation to cure.

FRESH ON THE SCENE
Six newer pumpkin varieties to try.

1. BLUE PRINCE
These large flattened blue-gray pumpkins are both decorative and delicious. Use the roasted creamy flesh in favorite fall recipes.

2. TOAD
The compact plant, perfect for small gardens or containers, produces five to six small bright orange pumpkins covered with large bumps.

3. SILVER EDGED

The vine yields a heavy crop of fruits with green and silvery white stripes. The pumpkins are 5 to 8 pounds and packed with large seeds for roasting.

4. LEMONADE

This pumpkin's golden skin adds a new hue to autumn decor.

5. SHIVER

Compact pumpkins with ghostly pale skin and a round shape grow on a bush-type plant ideal for small spaces.

6. BLANCO

These smooth white pumpkins are deer resistant and just the right size for small jack-o'-lanterns.

Direct Sow to Save Time

Skip starting seeds indoors and put the goods right into the ground.

gives you more options than relying on what's available at most local garden centers. But if starting seeds indoors feels daunting, take advantage of the many vegetable and flower seeds that perform just as well when set right in the ground. Here's how to have the best success with direct sowing.

Track Your Last Frost

Direct sowing usually works only when you plant after your area's last frost date. According to Burpee, one of the biggest seed retailers, that date may vary quite a bit over a short geographic distance. If you're not entirely sure what that date is for your neighborhood, ask an experienced gardener or someone at your local extension office. Also make sure the plants you've chosen have time to reach maturity in your growing season.

Prep the Soil

Pull any vegetation left from last year. Then loosen the soil—break up clumps and remove sticks and rocks—as much as possible so seeds can easily send down their roots.

Bean sprouts

Mix in compost or manure to provide nutrients that growing plants need.

Sow the Seeds
If seeds are small, such as carrot, mix them with some sand to make it easier to disperse them evenly. Sow them along the surface, and then cover them lightly with commercial seed-starting mix. Tuck large seeds, such as beans, into the soil at the depth recommended on the packet.

Water Often
Just be gentle. Use a light setting on your hose sprayer to water the seeds thoroughly without washing them away. As seeds begin to sprout, try to keep the soil consistently moist. You may even need to water twice a day, depending on your location.

Mark the Plantings
Busy gardeners know it's easy to forget what seeds you've planted where. Use string to mark your rows from above until you notice sprouting. Use plant markers at the heads of rows or sections. Save the seed packets to refer to them later, in case you have questions.

Thin Those Seedlings
It's exciting to see all your direct sow seeds sprouting. Just keep in mind: Any growing too close together won't thrive. Follow the instructions on the original packet to thin seedlings to the advised spacing. Keep only the strongest seedlings. Pinch the others off at the base. It's important not to pull them, or you could dislodge the roots of others nearby.

BEST PLANTS FOR DIRECT SOWING
These favorites flourish when put right in the ground.

VEGETABLES	FLOWERS & HERBS
Beans	Columbine
Beets	Cosmos
Carrots	Dill
Corn	Larkspur
Lettuce and other greens	Marigold
Melons	Morning glory
Okra	Poppy
Peas	Snapdragon
Radishes	Sunflower
Spinach	Sweet pea
Turnips	Zinnia

Easy-to-Grow Natives

Attract birds, butterflies and more with American beauties.

1

Red admiral butterfly on native aster

1. Wild aster

SYMPHYOTRICHUM SPP., ZONES 3 TO 9

The world of native late-summer asters is a big one, with dozens of species that come mostly in shades of blue-purple. All are irresistible to butterflies, native bees, honeybees and a variety of other insect visitors. Heart-leaved, blue wood, smooth, New England, and white heath aster are adaptable and easy to care for. Research what's native to your area.

Why we love it: Aster shrugs off light frost and keeps the pollinators coming back for more.

2. Orange coneflower

RUDBECKIA FULGIDA, ZONES 3 TO 9

A long-blooming eastern native, orange coneflower is easy to recognize. Try out the cultivar Little Goldstar. Its blooms sprout from gorgeous dark green foliage. At about 16 inches tall, the flowers beckon butterflies from summer to fall. Not to mention that the seeds are a treat for birds in fall and winter, or as long as they last.

Why we love it: The bright color and long bloom time make this coneflower a standout.

3. Dense blazing star

LIATRIS SPICATA, ZONES 3 TO 9

Showy in both color and form, this eastern species flaunts vibrant fuzzy wands that stand 3 to 5 feet on tufts of grasslike leaves. It grows in moist meadows or near marshes, but it flourishes in average garden soil, too.

Why we love it: Blazing star brings in big butterflies! It's a magnet for monarchs and tiger swallowtails, and you also just might catch a glimpse of red admirals, painted ladies and sulphurs.

4. Virginia bluebells

MERTENSIA VIRGINICA, ZONES 3 TO 9

This spring wildflower of the East and Midwest makes a perfect companion for daffodils and hostas, then dies back until the next spring. Plant in humus-rich moist soil in sun to shade, where it will self-sow into a colony.

Why we love it: Its beauty would be reason enough, but this bloom is also a reliable nectar source for bees and other early spring pollinators.

5. Switchgrass

PANICUM VIRGATUM, ZONES 3 TO 9

Try a metallic blue variety of this Midwest prairie native, such as Heavy Metal Blue. Some types even boast red foliage in summer or fall. The dense clump of grass is topped by feathery seed heads in fall, with most plants reaching about 3 to 6 feet in bloom. It reseeds readily, so be sure to buy from a regional source.

Why we love it: Its vertical posture adds oomph to perennial beds with relaxed shapes.

6. Sunflower

HELIANTHUS SPP., ZONES 3 TO 9 OR ANNUAL

Despite cultivar names such as Russian Mammoth, all sunflowers have North or South American roots. About 70 species, both annual and perennial, are native from Canada into Mexico. Common sunflowers are easy to grow from seed, and may reach up to 10 feet tall.

Why we love it: In late summer, each bloom becomes a living bird feeder for chickadees, titmice, cardinals and others.

7. Adam's needle yucca

YUCCA FILAMENTOSA, ZONES 4 TO 10

Plant this southeastern eye-catcher in sun to part shade where you won't accidentally brush against its needle tips. *(Yee-ouch!)* It lives for decades, putting out pups to expand its 2-foot-tall clump of evergreen leaves. Flower stalks may reach up to 8 feet tall.

Why we love it: This yucca knows how to bring the drama, creating a powerful focal point with flower stalks on a spiky clump.

8. Wild red columbine

AQUILEGIA CANADENSIS, ZONES 3 TO 8

This 2- to 3-foot-tall plant of the eastern U.S. is a "This way!" sign for migrating hummingbirds. As spring moves north, ruby-throated hummers follow the red and yellow flowers of this nectar-rich perennial like hounds on a trail. The similar western version, *A. formosa,* is just as gratifying to grow.

Why we love it: Red columbine keeps blooming for months if you snip off the faded flowers.

9. Rocky Mountain penstemon

PENSTEMON STRICTUS, ZONES 4 TO 9

Possibly the easiest penstemon to grow, this Mountain West native spreads into a 2- to 3-foot mat in sun to part shade and dry soil. Flower stems arise in late spring and last into summer, with foliage persisting through the winter.

Why we love it: Bumblebees often crawl right into the plant's blossoms to drink nectar or to sleep, leaving their hind ends sticking out.

10. Plains coreopsis

COREOPSIS TINCTORIA, ANNUAL

The small bright flowers pack a big punch. This summer-through-fall bloomer—native to the Great Plains region of the central U.S.—is as easy to grow from seed as blue bachelor's button, which makes a beautiful companion. Research before you plant, as it can be invasive.

Why we love it: Native sparrows, juncos, goldfinches and other birds seek out the flower's seeds.

CHAPTER 7

Butterfly Life

Get up close to nature's winged works of art and see where they're likely to land.

Fluttering
Faves

Readers capture stunning
photographs of common
visitors—plus a few rarities.

My backyard is filled with native plants to attract bugs, birds and butterflies. The reward is observing the results of my efforts. I happened to find this great spangled fritillary fluttering around my blazing star and grabbed my Sony Alpha a6000. I like how the butterfly turned vertically to match the orientation of the flower spike.

Diane Spray
WAUSAU, WISCONSIN

The first flower on my dwarf sunflowers had just started to emerge when a painted lady butterfly stopped at this bloom. So I grabbed my Canon E0S Rebel T3i that I use to photograph wildlife, and I got this shot of two of my favorite things: sunflowers and wild butterflies.

Karen Thambyrajah
ST. PETERS, MISSOURI

Last September, I had the most special birthday gift. For the first time in more than 13 years, I spotted not one but three great purple hairstreak butterflies in my garden. I was elated, as these butterflies are gorgeous and I had only been able to photograph them once before. This one's colors were amazing as it sat on my sedum. The group stayed in my garden for several weeks. It was a very special month!

Laurie Stuchlik
MILTON, DELAWARE

Bidens plants grow at a county park near me along a lake, creating a yellow maze. Many pollinators just hover on the blooms, but this common buckeye stayed on the blossom for some time. I love its large, bold features, which pop against the yellow hues.

Sujata Roy
MORRISVILLE, NORTH CAROLINA

▲ My grandma grows a variety of pretty asters in her garden. One day when I was visiting her, clouded sulphur butterflies were everywhere. I always have my camera with me, so I sat among the flowers and waited for the fliers to settle down on purple coneflower blooms before taking this shot.

Katelyn Cheek
WASHINGTON, NEBRASKA

► A Gulf fritillary visited our Sapphire Showers duranta in the backyard. The detail in the butterfly's antennae and body, plus the crisp appearance of the blooms, make this photo special.

Dale Chellis
MELBOURNE BEACH, FLORIDA

I spotted this group of butterflies on a Meadow Blazing Star liatris last summer outside my hometown. I very rarely see this many monarchs on one plant, so I took a photo with my Canon E0S 5D Mark III and 150-600 Tamron lens.

Mary Carlson
PRINCETON, MINNESOTA

▶ In a prairie full of brightly colored swallowtails and monarchs, I took a moment to appreciate one of the smaller and less flashy butterflies, a cabbage white. The sun shining through its wings was a simple moment of beauty and a good reminder to stop and appreciate all the little things.

Mynette Jones
SPRINGBORO, OHIO

▼ It was a beautiful summer morning in Wisconsin, and I was walking in the field behind our yard when I saw this giant swallowtail. It fluttered around for quite some time, and I was able to get many photos of it. This is one of my favorites, even though the swallowtail is on an invasive cutleaf teasel. I can't get enough of these gorgeous butterflies!

Caron Gray
BROOKFIELD, WISCONSIN

An Epic Migration

There's more to the journey of monarchs than you may know.

THE FLIGHT OF THE monarch butterfly may seem like a straight-forward event, but it's anything but simple. The trip is complicated, involving several generations. Plus, there's both an eastern and a western migration, with many monarchs in the West wintering as far north as Santa Cruz, California. Take a look at the generation cycle for eastern monarchs (right) and the map of monarch flight paths (below) to better understand how this incredible event works.

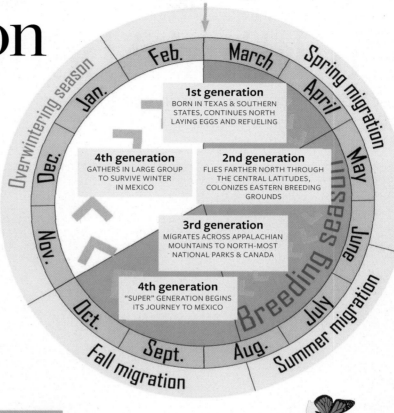

Breeding season begins

Overwintering season
Spring migration
Breeding season
Summer migration
Fall migration

1st generation
BORN IN TEXAS & SOUTHERN STATES, CONTINUES NORTH LAYING EGGS AND REFUELING

4th generation
GATHERS IN LARGE GROUP TO SURVIVE WINTER IN MEXICO

2nd generation
FLIES FARTHER NORTH THROUGH THE CENTRAL LATITUDES, COLONIZES EASTERN BREEDING GROUNDS

3rd generation
MIGRATES ACROSS APPALACHIAN MOUNTAINS TO NORTH-MOST NATIONAL PARKS & CANADA

4th generation
"SUPER" GENERATION BEGINS ITS JOURNEY TO MEXICO

Jan., Feb., March, April, May, June, July, Aug., Sept., Oct., Nov., Dec.

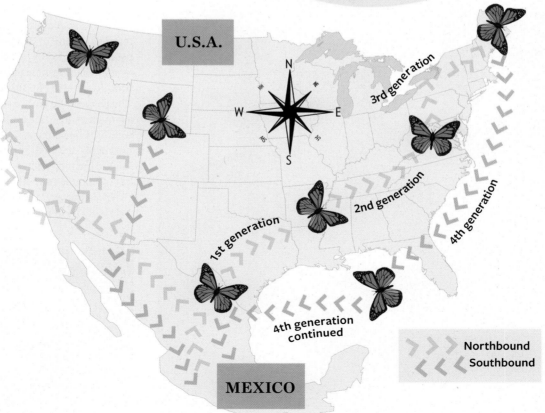

U.S.A.

3rd generation

2nd generation

1st generation

4th generation

4th generation continued

MEXICO

Northbound
Southbound

Puddlin' About

Discover the surprising reason butterflies are attracted to a bit of standing water.

Little yellows

MOST OF US ARE USED TO SEEING backyard butterflies flutter and dip between blooms in bright sunny gardens, dining on the sweet nectar that gives them the energy they need to survive. But occasionally you'll find butterflies in totally unexpected places, like mud puddles or the sandy banks of a river—sometimes gathering in extremely large groups. It may seem curious, but the butterflies, likely males, are engaged in an activity known as puddling.

"Male butterflies, just like any living creature, are trying to ensure that they reproduce," explains Ryan Fessenden of the Florida Museum of Natural History's Butterfly Rainforest. "One of the ways they're able to is by passing on nutrients, along with genetic material, to the females when they are mating."

When butterflies mate, males transfer a spermatophore to the females. Think of this as a tiny package that holds just about everything a female needs to produce healthy fertilized eggs. These spermatophores can make up as much as 10% of a male butterfly's weight. The package includes nutrients that help support the female butterfly's health, making her offspring more likely to survive.

"Male butterflies gather those nutrients by drinking water from

Eastern tailed-blue

Pipevine and eastern tiger swallowtails

wet spots on the ground, collecting minerals and nutrients like sodium and amino acids," Ryan says.

And it's not just the mud that attracts butterflies. Like other animals, butterflies need salt in their diet, and they find it in some unexpected spots. "You may find a butterfly seeking out valuable nutrients in some rather unusual locations, such as in the tears of a crocodile or the sweat of a human's skin," Ryan says. They are also drawn to less savory items, such as decaying flesh and excrement. There are even moths in Central America that puddle on blood.

Off-putting as it may seem, these behaviors are vital to a butterfly's survival. That's why you may see huge swarms of dozens or even hundreds of them when a good puddling spot appears.

"The more males that can gather nutrients, the more success the species will have reproducing," Ryan says. "So when a wet spot or puddle is found by one, others will notice and join in."

Any type of butterfly can puddle, but it's most common in whites, sulphurs and members of the swallowtail family. In particular, look for tiger swallowtails, red-spotted purples, white admirals, cabbage whites, and clouded and cloudless sulphurs at puddles. They are all there for one reason—to ensure they survive and thrive for many generations to come.

MAKE YOUR OWN PUDDLE STATION

Help butterflies, especially during dry weather, with a backyard puddling spot.

- Find and fill a shallow dish or container with soil or sand. Add a few flat rocks to provide perching spots.
- Pour enough water in the container to moisten the soil. Sprinkle salt on the surface. Also set out overripe fruit such as bananas and oranges.
- Keep the soil moist during the heat of daylight hours, when butterflies are more likely to visit.

Stripes in the Sky

Keep an eye out for the distinctive markings of the eastern tiger swallowtail butterfly, found throughout much of the U.S.

▲ I happened to look outside and saw this butterfly on my sunflowers. I quickly ran to take a photo.

Taylor Gailhouse
LAWTON, MICHIGAN

► This photo shows a lot of the butterfly's body. You can see its long legs, the antennae curving up above those big eyes, and the proboscis dipping into the flower.

Brenda Johnson
BOYDS, MARYLAND

◄ Photographing nature has brought me such joy. This swallowtail entertained me as it flitted over four lantana plants.

Jennifer Hardison
ATHENS, TENNESSEE

Green with yellow and black decoy eyespots, the eastern tiger swallowtail caterpillars have orange "horns" they can extend when they feel threatened.

EASTERN TIGER SWALLOWTAIL

WINGSPAN

3 to 5½ inches.

DISTINCTIVE MARKINGS

Four black parallel stripes at the top of each wing and a solid black stripe along the base. Females have more blue on the hind wings. A dark form looks similar to a pipevine swallowtail.

RANGE

Spans from the East Coast to the Great Plains.

HABITAT

Parks, suburbs, forests and fields.

HOST PLANTS

Wild cherry, tulip tree, cottonwood, sweetbay, willow and white ash.

EGGS

Females lay a large green egg on a host plant's leaf.

NECTAR FAVORITES

Milkweed, Joe Pye weed, wild cherry and lilac.

All-American Beauty

Search for this favorite taking flight.

Key ID clue! Look for white dots on the forewings.

▲ **I was just learning** to use my camera when I captured this gorgeous American lady butterfly on a white coneflower in my yard. Photography is a great hobby that allows me to get a closer look at the beauty of butterfly wings, which I could not see otherwise.

Deborah Billings
WATKINSVILLE, GEORGIA

◄ **Butterflies are one** of my favorite things to observe and photograph. Getting a picture of this American lady in my current home of North Carolina brings back childhood memories of my family farm in upstate New York.

Jason Baden
CHARLOTTE, NORTH CAROLINA

The caterpillar varies in coloring but is typically yellow or black with bands wrapping around its body. Look for white spots on the abdominal segments and large spines accented by reddish bases.

AMERICAN LADY

WINGSPAN
1¾ to 2⅝ inches.

DISTINCTIVE MARKINGS
A mixed pattern of mostly orange hues from above, including a small white spot within the orange. The underside of the hind wings have two large dark eyespots, setting it apart from the painted lady.

RANGE
Most of the U.S. and southern Canada.

HABITAT
Open areas, including fields and gardens.

HOST PLANTS
Plants from the *Asteraceae* family, including sweet everlasting, ironweed and pussytoes.

EGGS
Pale green.

In Plain Sight

Find cabbage white butterflies along roadsides, in gardens and beyond.

▲ **Cabbage whites are plentiful** here in the Midwest. My grandchildren absolutely delight in running after them.

Tara Steffen
BERNE, INDIANA

▶ **During an unusually warm day** in late September, I saw this butterfly posing on an aster with its wings wide open.

Trisha Snider
ST. THOMAS, ONTARIO

◀ **I captured this image of a delicate** cabbage white butterfly while on a morning walk along a field in Darlington, Wisconsin. It was enjoying some thistle flowers and stopped long enough for me to snap its photo.

Jennifer Kelly
FITCHBURG, WISCONSIN

Green with a faint yellow line along the tops of their bodies, these caterpillars munch on members of the cabbage family. Look closely and you might see fine white hairlike structures sticking up—they release chemicals and ward off ant attacks.

CABBAGE WHITE

WINGSPAN
1¼ to 1¾ inches.

DISTINCTIVE MARKINGS
Upper sides of wings are white. Forewings have one dark spot on males and two on females, as well as charcoal-colored tips.

RANGE
Native to Eurasia. Introduced to southern Canada and most of the U.S.

HABITAT
Common in most open areas.

HOST PLANTS
Members of the cabbage family, including broccoli and mustard plants.

EGGS
Females leave one egg on underside of leaf. Color changes from white to yellow.

NECTAR FAVORITES
Mustards and asters.

Backyard Safari

Zebra swallowtails add an element of adventure to any garden.

▲ **Every summer I think** I should pull up the aggressive gooseneck loosestrife flowers in my yard. But then butterflies, including this zebra swallowtail, enjoy them. It's a very large butterfly when you compare it to the loosestrife blooms.

Jill Crowe
NEWARK, OHIO

◄ **While I was taking photos of** dragonflies, I saw a beautiful zebra swallowtail sipping butterfly weed nectar. I adjusted the shutter speed of my Canon EOS 7D to freeze the action. I love that the photo shows off the red markings under the wing.

Mark Tegges
ELDERSBURG, MARYLAND

Zebra swallowtail caterpillars are mostly green with one thicker band of blue, black and yellowish close to the head. Thin yellow stripes accent the abdominal segments. Closer to hatching, caterpillars are darker.

ZEBRA SWALLOWTAIL

WINGSPAN
2½ to 4 inches.

DISTINCTIVE MARKINGS
Green-tinted white with black stripes and very long tails. Red accents visible from above and a red stripe on the underwings.

RANGE
South of New England down into Florida and west into Texas and Nebraska.

HABITAT
Woods to brushy fields.

HOST PLANTS
Pawpaw plants, favoring common pawpaw.

EGGS
Pale green, found on the tips of young leaves.

NECTAR FAVORITES
Seen in spring and summer, flying nearly year-round in the Deep South.

On the Vine

Dark and beautiful pipevine swallowtails are irresistable to watch.

I spotted this pipevine butterfly on some ironweed in our pasture in July. Several minutes passed as I watched it feed—then it fluttered away. I enjoyed observing as it went floating from flower to flower. I love this photograph and the memories it brings.

Carol Boykin
PETTY, TEXAS

Late summer is my favorite time to go for a walk in my local state park. I love to see butterflies home in on native thistle, and the pipevine swallowtail is one of my absolute favorites.

Patricia A. Winter
BECKLEY, WEST VIRGINIA

As the pipevine caterpillar grows, its appearance changes. It slowly becomes darker, with more pronounced dots of color and longer black tubercles, which look like antennae.

PIPEVINE SWALLOWTAIL

WINGSPAN
2¾ to 5 inches.

DISTINCTIVE MARKINGS
Blackish from above with deep blue hindwings and light dots. From below, dark with light markings and large orange dots.

RANGE
From southern Connecticut down to central Florida and west to Arizona, plus populations in California, Mexico and Ontario.

HABITAT
Open areas, including gardens.

HOST PLANTS
Plants from the genus *Aristolochia*, sometimes also called pipevines.

EGGS
Red-orange with small bumps.

CHAPTER 8

Ask the Experts

Our pros, Kenn and Kimberly Kaufman and Melinda Myers, fly in with answers.

Q Why does this tufted titmouse have an orange breast and neck?

RaDel Hinckley INDEPENDENCE, MISSOURI

Kenn and Kimberly: That's a fascinating bird. Normally the tufted titmouse is orange on the flanks and under the wings but pure white on the rest of the underparts and on the face. On some birds, the white is tinged with cream, buff or, very rarely, light orange. The bird in your photo is an extreme case. It's possible that it was stained by something such as decaying wood on a dead tree, but the color looks too even for that. We think it just has an unusual amount of carotenoid pigment (which causes a natural red or orange tone) in what otherwise would be white feathers.

Q What is this charming thing growing on my gatepost?

Madeleine Martin MOORES HILL, INDIANA

Melinda: This common lichen (*Cladonia cristatella*) is found in Canada and most of the northeastern U.S. Often called red caps or British soldiers because their tops resemble the red caps once worn by British troops, these slow-growing lichens are usually found on rotting wood and occasionally on the bases of healthy trees. Lichens are formed by a rare partnership between a fungus and algae or cyanobacteria. The role of the fungus is to provide protection, while the algae and cyanobacteria bring nutrients to the party.

Q. The amaryllis bulbs I store and regrow have red blotches on the leaves and stems. What's wrong with them?

Sue Gronholz
BEAVER DAM, WISCONSIN

Melinda: The symptoms match both the name and the description of a fungal disease called red blotch. It may develop at the base of flower stalks and emerging leaves. Infected leaves may become distorted, or the stalks could break easily. The disease isn't fatal, but it can ruin the plant's appearance. Reduce the risk of disease by buying healthy bulbs, using clean containers and planting in sterile potting mix. Prevent the spread by using rubbing alcohol to clean any tools and stakes used on the infected plants. If the disease persists, use a fungicide or replace the bulbs.

Q. This dark-eyed junco doesn't look like any others at my feeder. What kind is it?

Christi Bennett DEMOTTE, INDIANA

Kenn and Kimberly: With those rich colors, this dark-eyed junco is definitely a visitor from the West. Several western varieties of juncos have reddish brown or pinkish brown on the back and sides. They're put into the category of Oregon juncos. Of that group, the ones nesting in southern Montana and northern Wyoming are called pink-sided juncos. This doesn't look like a pure pink-sided because the hood is very dark, not the common pale blue-gray. It could be a cross between a pink-sided and another Oregon type. Regardless, it's exciting to see it among the slate-colored types that visit Indiana regularly.

Q Barred owls have raised young in our nest box for years but a gray squirrel moved in recently. Will the owls still use the box?

Sheldon Schall WAUNAKEE, WISCONSIN

Kenn and Kimberly: In a battle between a squirrel and a barred owl for a nest box, the owl will almost certainly be the victor. Squirrels may be able to displace a smaller owl, such as a screech-owl, but not one as large as the barred. In fact, although barred owls typically hunt smaller mammals, squirrels are also part of their diet. So when the owl returns, you can expect that squirrel to beat a hasty retreat.

Q This hummingbird stayed in my yard last winter. Is it a young male or an adult female rufous hummingbird?

Marci Jones MELROSE, FLORIDA

Kenn and Kimberly: Adult female and young male hummingbirds look very similar in some species, so it can be hard to tell the difference. Among rufous hummingbirds, adult females often have some red on the throat, but it tends to be concentrated in the center of the lower throat. Young males can show the same pattern, but they typically have larger red spots scattered around the throat. Your photo shows an individual with big red patches over the side of the throat as well as in the center, so we would call it a young male.

Q What kind of bird is this? I saw it in a swampy area.

Gail Jakubiak HUDSON, FLORIDA

Kenn and Kimberly: This yellow-rumped warbler is mainly a winter visitor in Florida, arriving in late fall and leaving in early spring. In this pose, most of its key field marks are hidden, including a yellow patch at each side of the chest and its trademark yellow rump patch. But it's recognizable by the contrast of its brown cheek patch, white throat and striped chest. While many warblers leave the U.S. to fly deep into the tropics in winter, yellow-rumped warblers can thrive in cold weather by eating berries.

Q I've been trying to feed dried mealworms to my bluebirds. How can I keep the worms from blowing away in the wind?

Rose Scaffidi DUNBAR, WISCONSIN

Kenn and Kimberly: Dried or alive, mealworms make a wonderful addition to the bird-feeding menu. Live mealworms are pricey and present the added challenge of keeping your investment from crawling away. While somewhat less appealing to birds, dried mealworms are less expensive and easier to store, and they won't go crawling off. To keep them from blowing away, mix them with birdseed in a high-sided tray to block the wind. Soaking them in warm, clean water, then draining and putting them in the feeder will make them heavier and less likely to blow away. Birds may also find them more appealing.

Q. I recently purchased a small water fountain. When should I run its timer?

Paula Ruelius ENOLA, PENNSYLVANIA

Kenn and Kimberly: The movement of water in a fountain is a delightful way to keep water circulating and fresh. Another important advantage is that the sound of the fountain may catch the attention of birds and help them find the water source. Since many small birds migrate at night or move around the landscape at dawn, early morning is the time that new birds are most likely to be passing through. We recommend setting the timer to start the fountain around sunrise to entice visitors to discover the water source and spend more time in your yard.

Q. Should we take down a nest left on our garage last year so a blue jay family can make a new one?

Barbara Lepkowski PLOVER, WISCONSIN

Kenn and Kimberly: Blue jays usually build nests in trees; nesting sites on buildings are less common. Sometimes a pair will spruce up an old nest and use it again or build a new nest in the same spot, but generally these birds don't. So if you want them to nest in the same place again, there isn't much you can do except wait and hope. Technically, under the Migratory Bird Treaty Act, it's illegal to remove the nests of most native species—even after the birds have finished using them—so that's another reason to leave the old nest where it is.

Q. I once saw a mass of yellow butterflies hovering in a sphere above a small tree. What was happening?

John Diaz BARHAMSVILLE, VIRGINIA

Kenn and Kimberly: Some insects engage in mating swarms. One example involves a group with the charming name of dance flies. In some species of dance flies, males gather above a shrub or other object, flying up and down and around while they wait for females to enter the dance. This kind of behavior is not typical for butterflies in your area, so you may have witnessed a highly unusual event.

Q. My grandmother called this a pic-a-back bush. What is it?

Susan Dufault LEWISTON, MAINE

Melinda: Plant lore passed from one generation to the next is part of both the fun and adventure of gardening. Common names such as the one that your grandmother provided are often limited to certain families or regions. Your grandmother's plant is a type of honeysuckle (*Lonicera*). The fused leaves near the growing tip and the cluster of flower buds are typical of several honeysuckle vines, including Italian honeysuckle (*L. caprifolium*). Once the flowers appear, it will be easier for you to identify the specific honeysuckle species.

Q. This bird stopped at our feeder with a flock of goldfinches. Is it a finch?

Elaine McCabe NEWPORT, NEW YORK

Kenn and Kimberly: The colors in birds' feathers are created by a few different categories of pigments, and these can be affected by various things. Black, gray and most of the brown colors in feathers are produced by melanins, while yellow, red and orange are produced by carotenoid pigments. The beautiful bird at your feeder looks like an American goldfinch that has normal carotenoid pigments (producing the bright yellow) but is lacking melanins. That's why it looks as if someone took a normal goldfinch and deleted all the black from its wings and tail.

Q For the first time we had four male grosbeaks at our feeder. How do we keep them coming back?

Laura Lisovich BELLE VERNON, PENNSYLVANIA

Kenn and Kimberly: A highlight of spring all over the East is the chance to see rose-breasted grosbeaks at feeders. During migration they stop over in practically any habitat, so in spring or fall keep your feeders filled with sunflower seeds to attract them. For their summer nesting season, however, they seek out areas with many mature trees, including forests and well-wooded suburbs and parks. Grosbeaks aren't likely to stay more than a few days in a spot without good forest cover, but you could make a long-term effort to attract them by planting more trees.

Rose-breasted grosbeak on sunflower feeder

Q Is it safe to put pennies in birdbaths to help limit algae growth?

Megan Long RED WING, MINNESOTA

Kenn and Kimberly: While it works to a point, algae eventually will grow. Pennies include other metals besides copper, and traces of those metals might contaminate the water and be harmful to birds. To keep your birdbath in suitable condition for your feathered guests, there's just no substitute for frequent cleaning.

Q What plant is this? It grew where some birdseed spilled.

Kathleen Carroll EASTON, MARYLAND

Melinda: This yellow-flowered mystery plant looks like mustard. The four petals that make up the flower, the cylindrical seedpods and the leaf shape are clues to its identity. Mustard plants are considered weeds by many gardeners. Some mustards are listed as noxious weeds, and others are used as cover crops. Birds may have deposited a few mustard seeds while visiting your feeders. I would recommend removing these plants as they appear and before they drop their seeds. That way, you'll prevent them from becoming a real nuisance in your garden.

Q Is this a red-tailed hawk?

Chris Almeida NEWARK, CALIFORNIA

Kenn and Kimberly: You're correct—this is a red-tailed hawk. These birds are fascinating for several reasons, including the fact that they have so many different plumage variations. Most are white on the chest, but some—especially in the West—are reddish brown or almost black on the underparts. This one is a beautiful example of what is often called the rufous morph. Here it's hard to see its tail color (one of the standard ways of telling adult red-tailed hawks from juveniles), but this one is definitely a juvenile because it has yellow eyes; adults are dark eyed.

Q Sparrows are mobbing my jelly feeder. How can I make sure my orioles get food, too?

Joan Webster CLARKSTON, MICHIGAN

Kenn and Kimberly: Unfortunately, any method to block sparrows from a jelly feeder would also block orioles. But if the sparrows become too much of a problem, you can temporarily switch out the jelly for oranges or a sugar-water feeder—orioles love both, and sparrows don't show much interest in either. Offering up oranges can be as simple as cutting them in half and impaling them on a branch. To offer sugar water, check out a bird supply store for feeders designed specifically for orioles. Some are made to supply both oranges and sugar water. Just be sure to select a feeder that's easy to clean.

Q. Are there any houseplants that fare better than others outside in summer in shady pots?

Kathy Eppers ALEDO, TEXAS

Melinda: Almost any houseplant can be grown outdoors during the summer as long as you have the growing conditions it prefers. Ivies, begonias, palms, elephant ears, asparagus ferns and true ferns are all good choices for shady locations. Gradually introduce your indoor plants to the more intense growing conditions outside. Check the soil moisture daily and adjust your watering schedule as needed.

Q. Rabbits ate all my marigolds. What are your suggestions for other colorful, long-blooming, rabbit-resistant annuals?

Peggy Connors NEWTON, NEW HAMPSHIRE

Melinda: I hesitate to list any plant as truly rabbit-resistant, since the eating habits of these critters can change when populations are high and their food is scarce. Though marigolds are often listed as rabbit-resistant, you discovered that this is not always the case. Something to keep in mind when reviewing any lists of rabbit-resistant plants: There will most likely be discrepancies. Ageratum, cleome, flowering tobacco, snapdragons and verbenas appear as rabbit-resistant on several lists. Zinnias appear on both susceptible and rabbit-resistant plant lists. Try a variety of plants. If rabbits decide to devour one type, the others can still provide needed color. Keep records of what works in your garden and be prepared to add new varieties as needed.

Q How do you handle the greenery after the flowers from spring bulbs are gone?

Joanne Tanner HAMBURG, NEW YORK

Melinda: It is best to leave the foliage intact and allow it to yellow and dry naturally. Try mixing the bulbs among perennials or planting annuals in bulb beds to help mask the fading leaves. Some gardeners braid the leaves to help hide them from view; others bend and bind them. These methods limit the amount of sunlight reaching the leaves, which means less energy is produced to support next year's blooms. Wait until the leaves fade to dig up the bulbs and store them in a cool dark place for summer. In fall you may want to replace some with new bulbs to boost the spring display and simply try something new.

Q What's this insect?
Laurie Putney
CAPE VINCENT, NEW YORK

Kenn and Kimberly: Members of the giant silk moth family are beautiful but not often seen, because the adults live just long enough to mate and lay eggs. This one has the pattern of a cecropia moth, which is widespread in eastern North America but usually shows more red in the wing stripes. Where you are in northern New York, you also might come across a related species, the Columbia silk moth. It is very similar to the cecropia moth but is smaller and usually lacks any hint of red in its pale wing stripes.

Q Do birds that have more than one brood per year reuse their nests?
Liza Peniston AUGUSTA, KANSAS

Kenn and Kimberly: There are endless variations in bird behavior but, as a very general rule, smaller birds usually make their nests for a single use, especially those that build nests in the open. For example, mourning doves, ruby-throated hummingbirds and robins usually (but not always!) build a new nest for each brood. But birds that build nests in enclosed spaces, such as bluebirds or house wrens that use tree cavities or birdhouses, are somewhat more likely to use those spots for a second brood. Large birds such as eagles or herons may return to the same nest year after year.

Q What is this lily-type flower?

Pat Given SANTA FE, TEXAS

Melinda: This unique climber, *Gloriosa superba*, goes by the common names gloriosa lily, climbing lily, cat's claw and several more. Hardy in Zones 9 and warmer, it's grown as an annual, or the tubers can be dug out in fall and stored indoors for winter in colder regions. This plant prefers full or filtered sun and rich, well-draining soil. Mulch the soil to keep roots cool and moist as temps climb. Tubers can be started indoors for earlier flowering or planted directly in the garden 2 to 4 inches deep after the last spring frost. Set the tubers horizontally in the ground, cover with soil, and water. Keep the soil moist throughout the growing season. It's important to note that all parts of this plant are poisonous, and it's considered invasive in parts of the U.S.

Q Is this a katydid? I've never seen a yellow one.

Siobhan Hutchison
BAILEY, MISSISSIPPI

Kenn and Kimberly: What a cool find! This is a very rare color form of the oblong-winged katydid, or *Amblycorypha oblongifolia*. They're typically green, but a few individuals can be pink, orange, tan, brown and, as you discovered, yellow. To answer your question as to whether or not it's a katydid requires a close look, and the answer is both yes and no. The oblong-winged katydid is actually considered a false katydid. You can distinguish it from a true katydid by its long forewings that extend beyond its hind wings when they're folded, which this image captures perfectly. The forewings of true katydids are much shorter. This is quite a special and exciting encounter.

Male ruby-throated hummingbird

Q A male ruby-throated hummingbird likes to zoom back and forth quickly while making a high-pitched chirping noise in my yard. What's he doing?

Kelly Kothenbeutel MAZEPPA, MINNESOTA

Kenn and Kimberly: Male ruby-throated hummingbirds put on impressive rituals called shuttle displays as part of their courtship behavior. A male quickly zooms from side to side in a shallow arc with his throat feathers flared out, making a loud whirring noise with his wings. This display is usually directed at a female, but she may be hard to spot if she's hidden in the foliage of a tree or shrub and is just watching without reacting.

Q Weeds have overtaken my mulched borders. I cleared them by hand and treated the area with vinegar, but they keep coming back. What should I do?

Pat Northington AUSTIN, TEXAS

Melinda: Vinegar just kills the tops of existing weeds. This may be enough to kill young seedlings, but it does not prevent weed seeds in the soil from sprouting. Also, since vinegar does not move from the leaves down into the roots, more established plants and perennials re-sprout from the roots of underground rhizomes. Several commercial organic herbicides use soaps and essential plant oils to kill weeds. Most just burn the leaves, are most effective on small plants and require repeat applications. Corn gluten meal may also help you keep weeds at bay. It's sold under several brand names as a treatment that prevents seeds from sprouting. Consider a combination of these options for best results.

Q I noticed woodpeckers have started to visit my hummingbird feeders. Is this common?

Pamela Swords BROWNSVILLE, KENTUCKY

Kenn and Kimberly: Many kinds of birds are known to visit sugar-water feeders. They seem to discover this food source by accident, but once they know about it, they keep coming back—and other species will copy them. In parts of the Southwest, where many people have hummingbird feeders out all year, this behavior is fairly common. It's more of a surprise in Kentucky, where you live. Now that your local woodpeckers have caught on, there's a good chance they'll keep visiting. The sugar water doesn't harm them, so it's just an interesting behavior to watch.

Q What type of butterfly is this?

Andrea Rickard HELENA, OHIO

Kenn and Kimberly: This is a good view of the intricate pattern on the underside of the wings of a hackberry emperor butterfly. The wings are also very strongly patterned on the upper sides, but with more of an orange-brown color. Hackberry emperors are widespread from the eastern states to as far west as Arizona. Interestingly, these butterflies seldom visit flowers. They're much more likely to show up near rotting fruit or a tree leaking sap.

Q My milkweed plants have curly leaves and deformed flowers. What went wrong?

Susan Nowicki WOODRIDGE, ILLINOIS

Melinda: Aphids are a very common milkweed pest. They suck plant juices and excrete the excess as a clear, sticky substance called honeydew. Their feeding can cause leaves to curl and, in some instances, distort the shape of the flowers. A black fungus often grows on the honeydew as well. This does not directly harm the plant, but in severe cases it can prevent sunlight from reaching the leaves. Consider waiting for natural predators such as lady beetles, parasitic wasps and green lacewings to move in and eat the pests. You can always give nature a hand, if needed, by dislodging them with a quick, strong blast of water from the hose.

Common milkweed

Q This butterfly landed on my coneflowers. What is it?

Mandy Dime FORT SMITH, ARKANSAS

Kenn and Kimberly: It's a rare species called the Diana fritillary, which flies in summer in a limited range in the southern Appalachians and the Ozarks. This black-and-orange individual is a male. A female has a similar pattern, but the orange is replaced by blue and white. As with other species of large fritillaries, their caterpillars feed on violet leaves.

Q I have a beautiful mountain ash tree, but for the last few years the fruit has dried up and fallen off prematurely. What's going on?

Marc White FAIRBANKS, ALASKA

Melinda: Hot, dry conditions can cause fruit, flowers and even leaves to dry up and drop from the tree. Review recent weather patterns to determine if this is the problem. It could also be scab, a fungal disease that causes spots to develop on the leaves and fruit. Severe cases can make the fruit drop. Clean up fallen fruit and leaves if this is the case. Tidying up and a little cooperation from the weather will help manage this disease. Fireblight, another potential cause, is a bacterial disease that can quickly kill whole branches or the entire tree. Pruning out infected branches beneath the affected area can slow the spread—just remember to disinfect your tools.

Baltimore oriole

Q How do you attract orioles to a suburban backyard?

Katie Pauer GAITHERSBURG, MARYLAND

Kenn and Kimberly: The strategy for attracting orioles is similar no matter where you live. Start by offering fresh fruit—healthy food that they love. Oranges and grapes are favorites. Many fruit feeders are available to purchase, but it can be as simple as slicing an orange in half and impaling the halves on a branch. Orioles also love sugar water, and there are feeders made specifically for them. If you plan to go the sugar-water route, make it yourself with 6 parts water to 1 part white sugar. Skip the orange dye and other ingredients—they're not needed and could harm the birds. Orioles also love grape jelly, but it should be offered in limited amounts. Think of grape jelly as a treat rather than a meal.

Q Is there a way to keep wasps out of birdhouses?

Robert Talbert PAYSON, UTAH

Kenn and Kimberly: This can be a challenge. You should never use insecticides on birdhouses. If you're monitoring the house closely, you can remove wasp nests just after the wasps start to build them. Open up the birdhouse on a chilly night when the wasps are sluggish. One trick is to rub soap on the inside of the top of the box, making the surface slick so wasps can't attach their nests. You should only do this if the house is designed with the entrance hole at least an inch or two below the top to reduce the chance that birds could accidentally get soap on their feathers.

Male ruby-throated hummingbird

Q I read that hummingbird feathers are not the bright colors we see. Can you explain this?

Cheryl Curtiss TACOMA, WASHINGTON

Kenn and Kimberly: It's true. When we look at an Anna's or ruby-throated hummingbird, for example, we're not really seeing green pigment on their back feathers or red pigment on their throat feathers. Instead, those are structural colors. The feather itself is dull and dark, but is covered with transparent layers of particular shapes that operate like a prism. They bend the light and reflect back only certain colors. This is why the colors can seem to change, too. Those red throat feathers may look orange, gold or even green, depending on the angle of the light.

Q What's this strange-looking bug?

Carol Wells EFFINGHAM, ILLINOIS

Kenn and Kimberly: This fascinating creature, which is yellow and black like a bumblebee but hovers in front of flowers like a hummingbird, is actually a moth. It's a member of the sphinx moth or hawk moth family, called a snowberry clearwing (*Hemaris diffinis*). This species is widespread in North America, mostly east of the Rockies, and actively feeds at flowers in the daytime. Its caterpillars will feast solely on the leaves of snowberry and honeysuckle.

Q Something is eating the flowers off my red hot poker plant each year. What could it be and what should I do?

Brenda Cookus MIDLOTHIAN, VIRGINIA

Melinda: When large parts of a plant are missing, animals such as deer, rabbits, chipmunks or squirrels are usually the culprits. When just a few flowers disappear at a time, birds are often the ones dining on your plant. Try covering the plants with netting or row covers to see if this stops the damage. An organic, rain-resistant repellent such as Plantskydd will protect your plants from hungry critters but won't dissuade the birds.

Orange Blaze red hot poker

Q I photographed a bird that looks similar to a woodpecker. What species is it?

Jackie Kottke BRAINERD, MINNESOTA

Kenn and Kimberly: This tricky member of the woodpecker family is in a plumage that's not seen very often—it's a very young juvenile yellow-bellied sapsucker. While young woodpeckers of most species look similar to their parents, these juveniles look very different at first, with head and body feathers that are mostly brown. They gradually replace their brown feathers with fresh new ones. By the following spring they show the same black, white, red and yellow pattern as the adults. On the bird in your photo, the best clue for identification is the long vertical white patch on the wing.

Q How do I stop whatever is eating my hibiscus plants?

Mary Brigham
SPRING ARBOR, MICHIGAN

Melinda: Japanese beetles feed on hibiscus and many other plants, causing damage. Healthy plants will survive the nibbling but look unsightly. Watch for and remove these coppery green beetles that eat and mate throughout the day. Knock them into a can of soapy water or use a small hand-held vacuum to remove and eliminate them. An organic insecticide containing the bacteria *Bacillus thuringiensis galleriae* is now available to control these pests. This strain of bacteria is effective against Japanese and other types of beetles.

Q What's this bug I found in my garden?

Julia Worth
WEYMOUTH, MASSACHUSETTS

Kenn and Kimberly: You've spotted an insect that's heard more often than it's seen. It's a cicada known as the northern dog-day cicada (*Neotibicen canicularis*). This species belongs to the same family as the periodical cicadas that make headlines when vast numbers emerge once every 13 or 17 years. But dog-day cicadas have more modest numbers and shorter life cycles, living underground for just two to five years before they mature and come to the surface.

Q After putting out fresh sugar water, there were swarms of honeybees at my hummingbird feeder. How can I prevent this?

Brenda Cookus MIDLOTHIAN, VIRGINIA

Kenn and Kimberly: One simple way to discourage bees is to use a saucer-style feeder. Look for one where sugar water is in a dish at the bottom and hummingbirds can stick their bills down through the openings or ports on the top. Bees and wasps can't reach the liquid from above, so as long as the outside of the feeder is kept clean, they won't be attracted. With other styles of feeders, putting bee guards over the ports sometimes keeps the insects at bay. Bees and other pollinators are important to the ecosystem, so we should never use products that harm them.

Female ruby-throated hummingbird

Q I see a lot of female hummers at our feeders but no males. Why could that be?

James Hoover PITTSBURGH, PENNSYLVANIA

Kenn and Kimberly: A few factors could come into play. Some studies have found slightly more females than males in the population of adult ruby-throated hummingbirds. Males have somewhat different behavior, too. They often perch higher so they can watch for rivals and visit feeders only briefly. Females spend a longer time at feeders while they're facing the demands of raising young without the help of the males. And in late summer, adult males are far outnumbered by all the newly independent young hummers, which look almost the same as adult females. On the other hand, it may be just an odd coincidence at your feeders.

Q I call this my rainbow sherbet moth. What's it really named?

Alan Bowen HENDERSONVILLE, NORTH CAROLINA

Kenn and Kimberly: We think rainbow sherbet moth is a wonderful name! But officially, it's called lia rosy maple moth (*Dryocampa rubicunda*). It's one of the smaller and more colorful members of the royal silk moth family and is related to species such as the cecropia moth and luna moth. The color pattern of the adult is variable, but it usually features a broad yellow band bordered by pink, just like your photo. Their caterpillars are known to feed on the leaves of maples and oaks.

Grow for Your Zone

Find the number associated with your region,
and stick to plants that will thrive in your area.

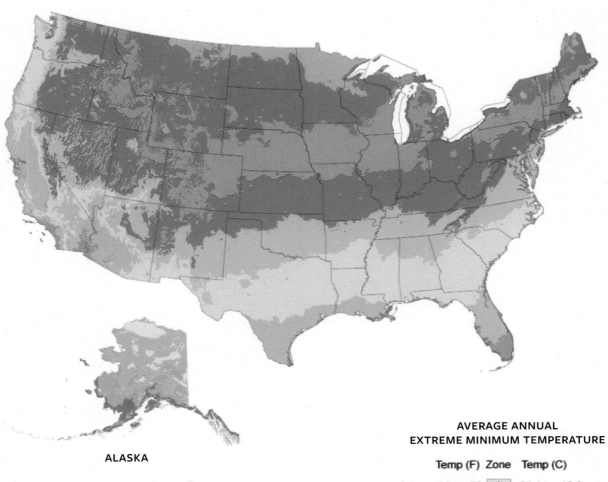

ALASKA

HAWAII

AVERAGE ANNUAL
EXTREME MINIMUM TEMPERATURE

Temp (F)	Zone	Temp (C)
-60 to -50	1	-51.1 to -45.6
-50 to -40	2	-45.6 to -40
-40 to -30	3	-40 to -34.4
-30 to -20	4	-34.4 to -28.9
-20 to -10	5	-28.9 to -23.3
-10 to 0	6	-23.3 to -17.8
0 to 10	7	-17.8 to -12.2
10 to 20	8	-12.2 to -6.7
20 to 30	9	-6.7 to -1.1
30 to 40	10	-1.1 to 4.4
40 to 50	11	4.4 to 10
50 to 60	12	10 to 15.6
60 to 70	13	15.6 to 21.1

USDA PLANT HARDINESS ZONES

Hardiness zones reflect the average annual
minimum cold temperatures for an area. If it's
difficult to precisely locate your city on the map
above, use the interactive version on the USDA
website, *planthardiness.ars.usda.gov*. Enter your
ZIP code, then your hardiness zone and average
minimum winter temperature range will appear.

Birdhouse Guidelines

Discover which dwellings are best for your backyard birds.

SPECIES	DIMENSIONS (LxWxH)	HOLE	PLACEMENT	COLOR	NOTES
Eastern bluebird	5"x5"x8"	1½" centered 6" above floor	5'-10' high in an open sunny area	light earth tones	likes open areas, especially facing a field
Tree swallow	5"x5"x6"	1½" centered 4" above floor	5'-8' high in the open; 50-100% sun	light earth tones or gray	within 2 miles of a pond or lake
Purple martin	multiple apartments 6"x6"x6"each	2⅛" centered 2¼" above floor	15'-20' high in the open	white	open yard without tall trees; near water
Tufted titmouse	4"x4"x8"	1¼" centered 6" above floor	4'-10' high	light earth tones	prefers to live in or near woods
Chickadee	4"x4"x8" or 5"x5"x8"	1⅛" centered 6" above floor	4'-8' high	light earth tones	small tree thicket
Nuthatch	4"x4"x10"	1¼" centered 7½" above floor	12'-25' high on tree trunk	bark-covered or natural	prefers to live in or near woods
House wren	4"x4"x8" or 4"x6"x8"	1" centered 6" above floor	5'-10' high on post or hung in tree	light earth tones or white	prefers lower branches of backyard trees
Northern flicker	7"x7"x18"	2½" centered 14" above floor	8'-20' high	light earth tones	put 4" of sawdust inside for nesting
Downy woodpecker	4"x4"x10"	1¼" centered 7½" above floor	12'-25' high on tree trunk	simulate natural cavity	prefers own excavation; provide sawdust
Red-headed woodpecker	6"x6"x15"	2" centered 6"-8" above floor	8'-20' high on post or tree trunk	simulate natural cavity	needs sawdust for nesting
Wood duck	10"x10"x24"	4"x3" elliptical 20" above floor	2'-5' high on post over water or 12'-40' high on tree facing water	light earth tones or natural	needs 3-4" of sawdust or shavings for nesting
American kestrel	10'x10"x24"	4x3" elliptical 20" above floor	12'-40' high on post or tree trunk	light earth tones or natural	needs open approach on edge of woodlot or in isolated tree
Screech-owl	10"x10"x24"	4'x3" elliptical 20" above floor	12'-40' high on tree	light earth tones or natural	prefers open woods or edge of woodlot

Note: With the exception of wrens and purple martins, birds do not tolerate swaying birdhouses. Birdhouses should be firmly anchored to a post, a tree or the side of a building.

Source: *Garden Birds of America* by George H. Harrison. Willow Creek Press, 1996.

Nest Boxes to Know

Welcome more bird families to your backyard with a variety of cozy places for them to raise their young.

WOODPECKER HOUSE

Entice woodpeckers with boxes attached to tree trunks, placing boxes 8 to 25 feet high. Add 4 inches of wood shavings to the floor for woodpeckers to use as nesting material. Vary the size of the entrance hole based on species: Downies like 1¼ inches; flickers favor 2½ inches.

SONGBIRD HOUSE

Chickadees, titmice, bluebirds and wrens are the most common backyard cavity nesters. They'll take up residence in classic wood birdhouses, but they're very particular about the size of the entrance hole. These songbirds are most likely to raise a family in a box if the hole is 1 to 1½ inches in diameter.

SCREECH-OWL HOUSE

Hang a box for screech-owls to nest in during summer and roost in during winter. They'll use a house with an elliptical entrance hole that's 4 inches wide by 3 inches high. Watch them peek their heads out near dusk. Bonus! Wood ducks enjoy the same type of birdhouse.

PURPLE MARTIN HOUSE

Purple martins nest in colonies, so consider a house with 6 to 12 cavities. Being a martin landlord takes some commitment, though. First set up a large multi-unit house 15 to 20 feet above ground, and then keep the cavities clear of nonnative house sparrows.

BUY OR BUILD

Find birdhouses at your local big-box store. Or look for a pattern online and make your own.

Birds and Their Favorite Foods

	Nyjer (thistle) seed	Cracked corn	White proso millet	Black oil sunflower seed	Hulled sunflower seed	Beef suet	Fruit	Sugar water (nectar)*
Rose-breasted grosbeak				●	●			
Black-headed grosbeak				●	●			
Evening grosbeak		●	●	●	●			
Northern cardinal		●	●	●	●		●	
Indigo bunting	●		●		●			
Eastern towhee	●	●	●	●	●			
Dark-eyed junco	●	●	●	●	●			
White-crowned sparrow	●	●	●	●	●			
White-throated sparrow	●	●	●	●	●			
American tree sparrow	●	●	●	●	●			
Chipping sparrow	●	●	●		●			
Song sparrow	●	●	●		●			
House sparrow	●	●	●	●	●			
House finch	●	●	●	●	●			
Purple finch	●	●	●	●	●			
American goldfinch	●	●	●	●	●			
Pine siskin	●	●	●		●			
Scarlet tanager							●	●
Western tanager							●	●
Baltimore oriole							●	●
Red-winged blackbird		●		●	●			
Eastern bluebird							●	
Wood thrush							●	
American robin							●	
Gray catbird							●	
Northern mockingbird							●	
Brown thrasher							●	
Ruby-throated hummingbird								●
Anna's hummingbird								●
Broad-tailed hummingbird								●
Tufted titmouse	●			●	●	●		
Black-capped chickadee	●			●	●	●		
White-breasted nuthatch				●	●	●		
Carolina wren						●		
Cedar waxwing							●	
Woodpecker				●	●	●	●	
Scrub-jay		●		●	●	●	●	
Blue jay		●		●	●	●	●	
Mourning dove	●	●	●	●	●			
Northern bobwhite		●	●		●			
Ring-necked pheasant		●	●					
Canada goose		●						
Mallard		●						

* To make sugar water, mix 4 parts water with 1 part sugar. Boil, cool and serve.
Store leftovers in the refrigerator for up to a week. Change feeder nectar every three to five days.

Source: *Garden Birds of America* by George H. Harrison. Willow Creek Press, 1996.

Choose a Seed Feeder

Use an option that attracts the birds you want to spot in your backyard.

HOPPER

This classic feeder is often in the shape of a house or barn and holds enough seed to feed birds for days. Hoppers are a surefire way to offer black oil sunflower seeds to finches, jays, cardinals, buntings and other perching birds. Many have suet cages on two sides, making them all-purpose feeders for every season.

TUBE

Tube feeders are available with small ports for thistle seed or larger ports for sunflower, safflower and mixed seeds. If you want to attract small, clinging birds such as chickadees, titmice and finches, look for a tube feeder with small perches under the ports. The perches discourage bully birds and squirrels.

THISTLE

Designed to hold tiny thistle seeds (also sold as Nyjer seeds), thistle feeders are a major draw for goldfinches. Feeders range from simple hanging mesh bags to plastic or metal tubes. You can even get ones that are a few feet long to feed an entire flock of finches or redpolls. Look for a thistle feeder that's easy to clean, as the small seeds can collect mold in enclosed tubes.

PLATFORM

These feeders hang from a tree branch or sit atop legs on the ground, and they are always completely open. This gives large birds enough space to land and eat. Sparrows, jays, juncos and blackbirds visit platform feeders, but so do squirrels.

Find feeders like these, and more, at a big-box store, garden center, specialty bird store or online.

Photography Credits

COVERS
Front: Steve and Dave Maslowski
Back: Diane Spray

INTERIOR
Alamy Stock: 6-7, 11 *bl* Nature Photographers Ltd.; **16** *b* Robert Harding; **23** William Leaman; **28** *b* Gina Kelly; **29** *tl* RF Company; **36** Khairil Azhar Junos; **64** John Van Decker; **76-77** Nature Picture Library; **94** *bl* Rick & Nora Bowers; **99** *bl* DPA Picture Alliance; **101** C-images; **109** *bl* AGAMI Photo Agency, *tr* James Mundy/Nature's Ark Photography; **173** *t* Rasvan ILIESCU; **205** *b* Rich & Nora Bowers
Alan Bowen: 234 *br*
Alan Murphy/BIA/Minden Pictures: 90 *t*
Alexander Videutsky: 11 *tr*
All-America Selections: 182 *t*
All Canada Photos Inc./Kevin G. Smith: 228 *r*
Amy Tripple: 216 *bl*
Andrea Rickard: 227 *l*
Ashley Maris: 18 *t*
Bailey Nurseries: 28 *tl*
Ball Horticulture Company: 164; 165 *tr*; 176 *b*; 187 *tl, tr*; 188 *bl, br*; 222
Barbara Clark: 20
Beth King: 39 *tl*
Bethany Terry: 223 *r*
Bob Kothenbeutel: 10; 14; 17; 81; 83 *b*; 91; 96 *t*; 98
Bob Walker: 109 *tl*
Bobbie Alexander: 65 *tl*
Brand X Garden Images: 158-159
Brian Zwiebel: 90 *b*
Bryan Reynolds: 200
Caleb Westering: 50-51; 58
Carl Bilancione: 60 *t*
Carol Boykin: 211 *t*
Carol L. Edwards: 220 *l*
Carol Wells: 231 *l*
Caron Gray: 198 *b*
Chris Almeida: 221
Christi Bennett: 215 *r*
Christine Haines: 47; 104-105; 111; 115 *br*; 119 *t*
Christine McCluskey: 22 *t*
Cindy Thompson: 78 *b*
Classic Brands: 49 *b*
Cobie Miller: 40 *tl*
Danny Brown: 2-3; 33; 110 *l*
Dave McCurry: 116 *b*
Dave Welling: 69
Deborah Billings: 205 *t*
Donald M. Jones/Minden Pictures: 13
Duncraft.com: 21 *b*; 22 *b*; 42; 49 *c*; 237 *tl, tr*; 239 *bl, br*
Elaine McCabe: 219 *r*
Encore Azalea: 167 *tr*
Francis & Janice Bergquist: 16 *t*; 48 *t*; 79; 108

Gail Buquoi: 32 *tl*
Gail Jakubiak: 212-213; 217
GAP Photos: 54-55 Friedrich Strauss; **156**; **178** *l* Marcus Harpur, *r* Visions; **179** Robert Mabic
Getty Images: 4, 153 northforklight; **27** *tr* saraTM, *tl* Feifei Cui-Paoluzzo; **29** *b* Galina Sandalova; **39** *b* Elizabeth W. Kearley; **41** stu99; **44-45** johann schumacher; **49** *tl* Steve Byland; **52-53** HannamariaH; **54-55** *br* skodonnell; **67** *tr* dmf87; **68** Monica Lara; **70** Mason Maron; **74-75, 80** *t* Neal Mishler, *b* miralex; **85** Jim Cumming; **99** *br* unew; **102** Marc Latremouille; **107** *tl* Design Pics/David Ponton; **110** *r* Keelyn Heaven; **115** *t* Art Wolfe, *bl* Zocha_K; **117** Adam Jones; **118** Jacques-Andre Dupont; **119** *b* Sjo; **157** focus35; **162** *tl* graphicdna, *bl* Tetiana Garusha; **163** *tr* rfisher27, *b* Kseniia Soloveva; **168-169** RossHelen; **154-155, 170-171** fatcamera; **172** Evan Sklar; **173** *br* Juj Winn; **175** *tl* Ed Reschke, *tr* Tim Grist Photography, *b* SvetlanaKlaise; **176** *tl* AntiMartina, *tr* Ed Reschke; **177** *b*, **186** Jacky Parker Photography; **180-181** eyewolf; **184** *r* hudiemm; **185** cjp; **187** *b* Michelle Shinners; **189** *tr* David H. Carriere, *tl* chapin31, *b* schnuddel; **207** *b* Maureen P Sullivan; **233** theresajam1; **236** malerapaso
Glenn Bartley: 89 *b*; 94 *tr*
Harris Seeds: 182 *b*; 183 *t, b, br*
Heathoutdoorproducts.com: 237 *br*
Jackie Kottke: 232 *l*
JB Smith: 61 *t*
Jeff Weymier: 48 *b*
Johann Schumacher Design: 8 *b*; 84; 96 *b*
John Gill: 30; 37; 56-57; 73; 116 *t*; 229
John Hamer: 60 *b*
Johnnyseeds.com: 183 *cr*
Joseph Bilinski: 59 *r*
Julia Worth: 232 *r*
Karen Thambyrajah: 5 *r*
Kathleen Carroll: 220 *r*
Kathy Adams Clark/KAC Productions: 107 *tr*
Kathy Banich: 62 *b*
Kimberly Kaufman: 103
Krista Kuskye: 234 *t*
Larry Ditto: 114, 115 *c*
Laurie Putney: 223 *l*
Lisa Kordes: 71
Longfield-gardens.com: 174
Madeleine Martin: 214 *b*
Mandy Dime: 228 *r*
Marie Read: 15; 82; 106
Marc Clark: 218
Marci Jones: 216 *r*
Meg Kolodick: 46 *tl*
Monrovia/Doreen Wynja: 167 *tl, b*
Mynette Jones: 198 *t*
Nancy Harmon: 61 *b*
National Park Service/S. Sparkhawk: 199

Nature Picture Library: 100
Nevin Hayter: 21 *t*
North States Industries, Inc: 18 *b*
Pat Given: 224 *l*
Patricia Welch: 8 *t*
Patricia Winter: 210
Peggy Booth: 226
Perkypet.com: 63; 72; 239 *tl*
Peter Darcy: 225
Provenwinners.com: 29 *tl*; 66; 165 *tl, b*; 166 *tl, b*; 167; 177 *tl*
RaDel Hinckley: 214 *t*
Richard Buquoi: 12; 14; 95
Richard Day/Daybreak Imagery: 78 *tl*; 201; 211 *b*
Rick Kleinosky: 153 *l*
Rolfnussbaumer.com: 24-25; 32 *tr*; 86 *b*; 88 *b*; 92; 94 *tr, br*; 97
Sandra Cooper: 227 *r*
Shutterstock: 26 Danita Delimont; **27** *b* guentermanaus; **28** *tr* Adam Gladstone; **65** *tr* Luiz Franco, *b* KajzrPhotography; **67** *tl* imageBROKER.com, *b* John A. Anderson; **83** *tl* Ian Dybal; **160-161** Switlana Sonyashna; **162** *br* New Africa; **184** *l* Marek P; **209** *b* Kevin Collison
Siobhan Hutchison: 224 *r*
Songbird Essentials, lookerinc.com: 237 *bl*
Star Roses and Plants: 166 *r*
Steve and Dave Maslowski: 9; 19; 31; 34-35; 38; 39 *tr*; 43; 46 *tr*; 86 *t*; 87; 88 *t*; 89 *c*; 93; 109 *bl*; 112-113; 230
Sue Gronholz: 215 *l*
Sujata Basu: 239 *tr*
Susan Dufault: 219 *l*
Susan Goewey: 40 *tr*
Susan Williamson: 62 *t*
Terra Nova Nurseries: 177 *tr*
Travis Bonovsky: title page
Tricia Snider: 203 *b*
U.S. Department of Agriculture: 235
Visions BV, Netherlands/VisionsPictures & Photography: 163 *tl*
Walter's Gardens, Inc: 188 *b*; 231 *r*
Wbu.com: 49 *tr*